Demonetization, Digital India and Governance

Demonetization,
Digital India and Governance

By

Niranjan Sahoo
Associate Professor,
Department of Rural Management,
Xavier Institute of Social Service (XISS), Ranchi

and

Sarika R. Lohana
UGC-Dr. Radhakrishnan Post-doctoral Fellow
in Humanities and Social Sciences,
School of Commerce and Management Sciences,
Swami Ramanand Teerth Marathwada University, Nanded

New Century Publications
New Delhi, India

NEW CENTURY PUBLICATIONS
4800/24, Bharat Ram Road,
Ansari Road, Daryaganj,
New Delhi - 110 002 (India)

Tel.: 011-2324 7798, 4358 7398, 6539 6605
Fax: 011-4101 7798
E-mail: indiatax@vsnl.com • info@newcenturypublications.com
www.newcenturypublications.com

Editorial office:
LG–7, Aakarshan Bhawan,
4754-57/23, Ansari Road, Daryaganj,
New Delhi – 110 002

Tel.: 011-4356 0919

First Published: **2017**

ISBN: **978-81-7708-441-2**

Published by New Century Publications and printed at Salasar
Imaging Systems, New Delhi.

Designs: Patch Creative Unit, New Delhi.

PRINTED IN INDIA

About the Book

The International Monetary Fund has hailed India as a *bright spot* amidst a slowing global economy. Indian economy has the potential to achieve double-digit growth rate.

In spite of being a *bright spot* on the world map, a host of problems confront India which caste shadow on its governance credentials. These so-called *black spots* include: (a) black money, (b) corruption, (c) money laundering, (d) counterfeit currency, (e) tax evasion and (f) terrorist financing.

The new Government at the Centre, which took charge in May 2014, under the dynamic leadership of Prime Minister Shri Narendra Modi has a vision to make India a modern and vibrant economy. Policies and programmes to rejuvenate the economy have already been announced in this regard.

It was in the above context that the Government of India decided to withdraw the legal tender character of ₹ 500 and ₹ 1,000 banknotes of the Mahatma Gandhi Series from the midnight of November 8, 2016. The announcement was made by no less a person than the Prime Minister himself in an unscheduled live televised address to the nation on the evening of November 8, 2016. The demonetized bank notes accounted for 86 percent of the country's cash supply.

The use of digital technology—world's fastest growing economic activity—to improve governance cannot be over-emphasized. Digital technology has become the greatest agent of change and promises to play this role even more dramatically in future. One major objective of the demonetization exercise is to encourage cashless/electronic transactions in the economy. The Government of India has taken policy decision to encourage electronic transactions and has, in this regard, announced a number of incentives.

Technology, competition, and benchmarking to the best international practices have to be the driving force of India's development efforts. Demonetization exercise needs to be seen in this perspective.

About the Authors

Dr. Niranjan Sahoo is currently Associate Professor in the Department of Rural Management, Xavier Institute of Social Service (XISS), Ranchi. He did his M.A. from Visva-Bharati Central University, Santiniketan, West Bengal; M.Phil. from BANISS (an ICSSR Institute), University of Indore; and Ph.D. from Magadh University. He also holds STC on Human Resource Management from IIT-Kharagpur.

He is the recipient of many awards, notably International Intellectual Achiever's Award conferred in Bangkok, Thailand (December 30, 2010); Visva-Bharati Snattakottar Award conferred by the then Prime Minister Shri I.K. Gujral (January 11, 1997); Rashtriya Gaurav Award (April 9, 2010) and Rajeev Gandhi Excellence Award (September 9, 2010). Recently, he was selected as a member to the Apex Committee of Uranium Corporation of India Limited (UCIL), Department of Atomic Energy, Government of India. Dr. Sahoo has visited a few South Korean universities also, viz. University of Suwon, University of Sinhan, Vision University, Hwashin Cybercity University and Chanbuk National University as guest professor.

He has published a number of research papers in academic journals of repute including *International Journal of Multi-Disciplinary Education and Research*, and *Journal of International Centre for Economics, Humanities and Management*, Bangkok. His areas of research interest include rural financial services, corporate social responsibility (CSR), entrepreneurship development, and human resources management.

Dr. Sarika R. Lohana is UGC-Dr. Radhakrishnan Post-doctoral Fellow in Humanities and Social Sciences, School of Commerce and Management Sciences, Swami Ramanand Teerth Marathwada (SRTM) University, Nanded. She received her M.Com. from SRTM University, Nanded; M.Phil. in commerce from Alaggappa University, Karaikudi; Ph.D. from the School of Commerce and Management Sciences, SRTM University and MBA in finance from IGNOU, New Delhi.

She has published papers in *Indian Journal of Management Review; Global Journal of Multidisciplinary Studies* and *Asian Journal of Management Sciences*. She is a member of the International Technical Committee on Social and Human Sciences, WASAT, (USA). Her areas of research interest include financial and marketing management, entrepreneurship, six sigma, corporate finance, neuro and behavioural finance.

Contents

Preface

The International Monetary Fund has hailed India as a *bright spot* amidst a slowing global economy. The World Economic Forum has said that India's growth is *extraordinarily high*.

Indian economy has the potential to achieve double-digit growth rate. However, this achievement hinges critically on: (a) improvement of the domestic savings rate (including public savings), (b) increased public investment, (c) efficient, reliable and affordable infrastructure, (d) higher inflow of foreign capital, (e) better credit delivery system, (f) labour reforms, (g) reduction in transaction costs, (h) improvement in technology and quality, and (i) export competitiveness.

The new Government at the Centre, which took charge in May 2014, under the dynamic leadership of Prime Minister Shri Narendra Modi has a vision to make India a modern and vibrant economy. Policies and programmes to rejuvenate the economy have already been announced in this regard. These have included, *inter alia*, Start-up India Initiative, 2016, eBiz Project, Make in India Campaign, Stand-Up India Scheme, Ease of Doing Business, India Aspiration Fund (IAF), Atal Innovation Mission (AIM), India Inclusive Innovation Fund (IIIF), Digital India, Smart Cities Mission, Atal Pension Yojana (APY) and permission to set up payment banks.

In the modern world, digital networking and communication infrastructures provide a global platform over which people and organizations devise strategies, interact, communicate, collaborate and search for information. It is widely accepted that the growth of the digital economy has widespread impact on the whole economy.

India has emerged in recent years as the most preferred destination for outsourcing of IT services. The vibrant IT industry is contributing immensely by providing information about latest technology and international business practices. IT has been contributing substantially to the economic growth of the country. More importantly, it can immensely help in accelerating the growth momentum by enhancing efficiency, competitiveness and technological edge across sectors, including particularly strategic sectors. Equally significant is the contribution of IT in enabling inclusive growth and development, and in ensuring that people across the length and breadth of the country have access to the opportunities generated by growth.

Indian economy has matured in several important respects. It is now much more integrated with the world economy and has benefited from this integration in many ways. The outstanding success of IT and IT-enabled services (ITES) has demonstrated what Indian skills and enterprise can do, given the right environment. Similar strength is now evident in sectors such as pharmaceuticals, auto components and, more recently in textiles. These gains in competitiveness need to be spread to other sectors.

In spite of being a *bright spot* on the world map, a host of problems confront India which caste shadow on its governance credentials. These so-called *black spots* include: (a) black money, (b) corruption, (c) money laundering, (d) counterfeit currency, (e) tax evasion, and (f) terrorist financing

Prime Minister Shri Narendra Modi has, time and again, reiterated his committed to eradicate the menace of black money. The very first decision of the Prime Minister-led NDA Government was the formation of a Special Investigation Team (SIT), soon after assuming office on May 26, 2014. A law was passed in 2015 on disclosure of foreign bank accounts. In August 2016 strict rules were put in place to curtail *benami* transactions. During the same period a scheme to declare black money was introduced. Prime Minister raised the issue of black money at the global forums, including multilateral summits and bilateral meetings with world leaders.

It was in the above context that the Government of India decided to withdraw the legal tender character of ₹ 500 and ₹ 1000 banknotes of the Mahatma Gandhi Series from the midnight of November 8, 2016. The announcement was made by the Prime Minister himself in an unscheduled live televised address to the nation on the evening of November 8, 2016.

The demonetized banknotes accounted for 86 percent of the country's cash supply.

Prime Minister assured the people that these decisions would fully protect the interests of honest and hard-working citizens of India and that demonetized ₹ 500 and ₹ 1000 bank notes hoarded by anti-national and anti-social elements would become worthless pieces of paper. He reiterated that the steps taken by the Government would strengthen the hands of the common citizens in the fight against corruption, black money and counterfeit notes.

In his address the Prime Minister shared the insight into how the magnitude of cash in circulation was linked to inflation and how the inflation situation was worsened due to the cash deployed through corrupt means. He added that it adversely affected the poor and the neo-middle class people.

The use of digital technology—world's fastest growing economic activity—to improve governance cannot be over-emphasized. It is transforming resource-based economies to knowledge-based economies. Digital technology has become the greatest agent of change and promises to play this role even more dramatically in future. It is changing every aspect of human life, apart from impacting changes in the field of communications, trade, manufacturing, services, culture, entertainment, education, research and national security. Digital technology has broken old barriers and is building new interconnections in the emerging concept of a single global village. It has also become one of the critical indicators of the progress of nations, communities and individuals.

Digital technology offers opportunities to overcome historical disabilities. It is a tool that will enable nations to achieve the goal of becoming a strong, prosperous and self-confident state. It promises to compress the time it would otherwise take for countries to advance rapidly in their march towards faster development.

One major objective of the demonetization exercise is to encourage cashless/electronic transactions in the economy. In recent years, advancements in banking technology, progress in mobile banking and innovative technologies to facilitate digital payments have enabled large number of small denomination transactions to be handled smoothly in electronic mode. The Government of India has taken policy decisions to encourage electronic transactions and has, in this regard, announced a number of incentives.

Technology, competition, and benchmarking to the best international practices have to be the driving force of India's development efforts. Hence, the various economic policies and programmes of the visionary Prime Minister Shri Narendra Modi should be seen in this perspective.

January 2017   **Niranjan Sahoo**
                                                 Sarika R. Lohana

Explanation of Select Terms Used Frequently in Financial Digitization

Aadhaar Payments Bridge System (APBS): APBS enables the transfer of payments from Government and Government Institutions to Aadhaar-enabled accounts of beneficiaries at banks and post offices.

Aadhaar-enabled Payment System (AEPS): AEPS is a bank led model which allows online interoperable financial inclusion transaction at PoS (MicroATM) through the Business Correspondent of any bank using the Aadhaar authentication.

Algorithms: Algorithms are essentially a set of well-defined finite sequence instructions used towards finishing a task. Algorithms are used extensively in computer science, bio-informatics, mathematics et al for calculation, data processing and other tasks.

Bandwidth: In the realm of computer networks, bandwidth refers to the capacity of data/information which can be carried through a channel (typically from website or server) in a given time interval. Bandwidth is thus a synonym for data transfer.

Benami Property: Benami (without a name) property refers to property purchased by a person in the name of some other person. The person on whose name the property is purchased is called the *benamdar* and the property so purchased is called the *benami* property. The person who finances the deal is the real owner.

Black Money: There is no uniform and universally acceptable definition of black money in fiscal literature. Generally speaking, the term *black money* stands for money earned by illegal means and kept secret and unaccounted for. It is widely used for smuggling activities, hoarding of scarce commodities, bribing government officials, financing political activities, and ostentatious living. Secret business deals through black money in turn lead to tax evasion and a vicious circle is created in which one evil thrives on the other. The term *black money* has many synonyms including *underground economy*, *parallel economy*, *shadow economy unofficial economy, and unaccounted economy*. All these terms usually refer to any income on which the taxes imposed by government or public authorities have not been paid. Thus, *black money* can be defined as assets or resources that have neither been reported to the public authorities at the time of their generation nor disclosed at any point of time during their possession.

Broadband: Broadband is a word that is tossed up every now and then when talking about internet and telecom. To download games, checking on your Twitter or Facebook profile or watch video all you need is internet broadband connection. A broadband channel is able to carry multiple signals. The overall capacity is divided into multiple, independent bandwidth channels with each channel operating on a specific frequency range. A broadband is also known as a high-speed internet service.

Browser: A browser is a user agent or a software that allows a user to search, access and interact with different types of information on the web.

Cloud Computing: Cloud computing is an emerging IT delivery model characterized by the new-age, internet-driven economics for increasing the capacities or adding capabilities without investment needs in infrastructure, training or software licensing. Today, cloud computing is the new lingo for all the IT executives. In cloud computing, cloud is only a metaphor. It refers to the range of servers located remotely which hosts computing applications.

Credit Card: It is a payment card issued to users (cardholders) to enable the cardholder to pay a merchant for goods and services, based on the cardholder's promise to the card issuer to pay them for the amounts so paid plus other agreed charges. The card issuer (usually a bank) creates a revolving account and grants a line of credit to the cardholder, from which the cardholder can borrow money for payment to a merchant or as a cash advance.

Crypto Currency: A crypto currency is a type of digital token that relies on cryptography for chaining together digital signatures of token transfers, peer-to-peer networking and decentralization. In some cases, a proof-of-work scheme is used to create and manage the currency.

Debit Card: It is a plastic payment card that can be used instead of cash when making purchases. It is similar to a credit card, but unlike a credit card, the money comes directly from the user's bank account when performing a transaction.

Dematerialisation (Demat): Demat is the process by which the physical certificates of an investor are converted to an equivalent number of securities in electronic form and credited in the investor's account with his depository participant (DP).

Demonetization: Demonetization is the act of stripping a currency unit of its status as legal tender. The process of demonetization involves either introducing new notes or coins of the same currency or completely replacing the old currency with new currency.

Depository System: Shares are traditionally held in physical (paper) form. This method has weaknesses like loss/theft of certificates, forged/fake certificates, cumbersome and time consuming procedure for transfer of shares etc. To eliminate these weaknesses, a new system called depository system has been established. A depository is a system which holds shares of an investor in the form of electronic accounts in the same way a bank holds money of a depositor in a savings account. A depository holds securities in dematerialised form. It maintains ownership records of securities in a book entry form and also effects transfer of ownership through book entry.

Digital Economy: It refers to an economy that is based on digital technologies. The digital economy is also sometimes called the *internet economy*, *new economy*, or *web economy*. Increasingly, the *digital economy* is intertwined with the traditional economy making a clear delineation harder.

Digital India: Vision 2019: Digital India is an initiative of the Government of India to integrate Government Ministries and their Departments with the people of India. It aims at ensuring the availability of government services to citizens electronically by reducing paperwork. The initiative also includes plans to connect rural areas with high-speed internet networks. Digital India has three core components. These include creation of digital infrastructure, delivering services digitally and digital literacy.

Digital Money (or Digital Currency): It can be defined as an Internet-based form of currency or medium of exchange which is distinct from physical currency (banknotes and coins), but allows for instantaneous transactions and borderless transfer-of-ownership. Both virtual currencies and crypto currencies are types of digital currencies, but the converse is incorrect. Like traditional money these currencies may be used to buy physical goods and services but could also be restricted to certain communities such as for example for use inside an on-line game or social network.

Digital Signature: A digital signature is the electronic signature issued by the certifying authority that shows the authenticity of the person signing the same.

Digital Wallet: It refers to an electronic device that allows an individual to make electronic transactions. This can include purchasing items on-line with a computer or using a smart phone to purchase something at a store. An individual's bank account can also be linked to the digital wallet. He may also have his driver's license, health card, loyalty card(s) and other ID documents stored on the phone. The credentials can be passed to a merchant's terminal wirelessly via near field communication (NFC).

Digitization: It is the process by which technology lowers the costs of storing, sharing, and analyzing data. This process has changed how consumers behave, how industrial activity is organized, and how governments operate.

E-filing of Returns: E-filing of income tax return is the process of electronically filing returns through internet which can be filed at any time at any place. While e-filing of income tax return is mandatory for a company and a firm liable to audit under Section 44AB of the Income Tax Act, 1961, it is optional for other assessees.

Electronic Banking (E-banking): E-banking is a generic term encompassing internet banking, telephone banking, mobile banking etc. In other words, it is a process of delivery of banking services and products through electronic channels such as satellite, telephone, internet, cell phone etc. The concept and scope of e-banking is still evolving. Internet banking is a major component of e-banking.

Electronic Commerce (E-commerce): E-commerce involves individuals and business organizations exchanging business information and instructions over electronic media using computers, telephones and other telecommunication equipments.

Electronic Money (E-money): E-money may be broadly defined as an electronic store of monetary value on a technical device used for making payments to undertakings other than the issuer without necessarily involving bank accounts in the transaction, but acting as a prepaid bearer instrument.

Electronically Know Your Customer (e-KYC): In the year 2013, RBI permitted e-KYC as a valid process for KYC verification under Prevention of Money Laundering (Maintenance of Records) Rules, 2005. In order to reduce the risk of identity fraud, documentary forgery and have paperless KYC verification, UIDAI has launched its e-KYC services. Under the e-KYC process—and after the explicit consent of the customer and after his or her biometric authentication from UIDAI data base—individual basic data comprising name, age, gender and photograph can be shared electronically with authorised users like banks, which is a valid process for KYC.

Hacking: It refers to the practice of breaking into a computer without authorisation, for malicious reasons, just to prove it can be done, or for other personal reasons.

Hawala: Hawala (reference/trust) is a popular and informal value transfer system based on the past record and honour of a huge network of money brokers—primarily located in the Middle East and the Indian subcontinent—operating outside of, or parallel to, traditional banking, financial channels, and remittance systems. In the most basic variant of the hawala system, money is transferred via a network of hawala brokers. It is the transfer of money without actually moving it or money transfer without money movement.

Immediate Payment System (IMPS): IMPS was launched by NPCI on November 22, 2010. It offers an instant, 24x7, inter-bank electronic fund transfer service through mobile phones as well as internet banking and ATMs.

Internet Banking: Internet banking offers different online services like balance enquiry, requests for cheque books, recording stop-payment instructions, balance transfer instructions, account opening and other forms of traditional banking services. These are mostly traditional services offered through internet as a new delivery channel. Banks are also offering payment services on behalf of their customers who shop in different e-shops, e-malls etc.

Internet Marketing: New forms of marketing also use the internet and are therefore called *internet marketing* or more generally *e-marketing, online marketing, digital marketing.* Internet marketing is sometimes considered to be broad in scope, because it not only refers to marketing on the internet, but also includes marketing done via e-mail, wireless media as well as driving audience from traditional marketing methods like radio and billboard to internet properties or landing page.

Internet Protocol: It refers to the set of techniques for transmission of data over the internet. Device connected to a network, internet or even a local area network (LAN) is assigned an internet protocol number. This address helps in unique identification of the device among all other devices which are connected to the extended network.

Legal Tender: Legal tender is any official medium of payment recognized by law that can be used to extinguish a public or private debt, or meet a financial obligation. National currency is legal tender in practically every country.

Micro-ATMs: Micro-ATMs are biometric authentication enabled hand-held devices. In order to make the ATMs viable at rural/semi-urban centres, low cost micro-ATMs are deployed at each of the *Bank Mitra* (Business Correspondent) location. This would enable a person to instantly deposit or withdraw funds regardless of the bank associated with a particular *Bank Mitra*.

Mobile Banking: The mobile phone revolution that is transforming the country could also turn into a banking revolution in terms of reach and transaction. The reach of mobile to the remote village and its usage by the common man has become order of the day. The coverage of mobile phones and the use of such instruments by all sections of the population can be exploited for extending financial services to the excluded population. It enables the subscribers to manage their financial transactions (funds transfer) independent of place and time. The subscriber can approach a retailer of mobile network for withdrawal/deposit of money and the transaction takes place using SMS messages.

Money Laundering: It is the process of transforming the proceeds of crime and corruption into ostensibly legitimate assets. In recent years, prevention of money laundering has assumed importance in international financial relationships.

National Electronic Funds Transfer (NEFT): NEFT is an electronic message-based payment system introduced by the Reserve Bank of India (RBI). It is a nation-wide retail electronic payment system to facilitate funds transfer by the bank customers, between the networked bank branches in the country.

National Financial Switch (NFS): NFS network started its operations on August 27, 2004. NFS is one of the several shared ATM networks which inter-connect the ATM switches of the banks together and thus enable inter-operability of the ATM cards issued by any bank across the entire network.

National Payments Corporation of India (NPCI): NPCI is an umbrella organization for all retail payments system in India. It was set up with the guidance and support of the Reserve Bank of India (RBI) and Indian Banks' Association (IBA).

National Unified USSD Platform (NUUP): It is an innovative service developed by NPCI and launched by the Indian Government in 2014. The service allows the banks and telecom service providers to work together seamlessly. The services of NUUP are based on the USSD method.

Real Time Gross Settlement (RTGS) System: RTGS system is owned and operated by the Reserve Bank of India (RBI). The system works on a mainframe computer. Members are provided with a participant interface (PI), using which the participants connect to the system at the RBI through the INFINET. The message flow architecture in the RTGS system uses the Y topology. The members communicate through their PI to the inter-bank funds transfer processor (IFTP) which validates all communication and also does the *strip and store* function.

Rematerialisation: Rematerialisation is the term used for converting electronic holdings back into certificates.

Remonetization: It is the opposite of demonetization and refers to restoration of a form of currency as legal tender.

Routers: Routers are physical devices in computer networking that are used to join together multiple wired or wireless networks. The work that a router performs is termed as routing. To put it in simple terms, routers are devices that facilitate computers to interconnect or communicate with other computers. Both wireless and wired routers are popular.

RuPay: RuPay is an Indian domestic card scheme conceived and launched by the National Payments Corporation of India (NPCI). It was created to fulfil the Reserve Bank of India's desire to have a domestic, open loop, and multilateral system of payments in India. In India, 90 percent of credit card transactions and almost all debit card transactions are domestic. However, the cost of transactions was high due to monopoly of foreign gateways like Visa and MasterCard. RuPay facilitates electronic payment at all Indian banks and competes with MasterCard and Visa in India.

Sniffing: It involves the use of a software program that is illicitly inserted somewhere on a network to capture ("sniff") user passwords as they pass through the system.

Spoofing: It refers to an attempt to gain access to a system by posing as an authorised user.

Unified Payment Interface (UPI) of India: UPI is a payment system which facilitates the fund transfer between two bank accounts. This payment system works on the mobile platform. Sending money through the UPI app is as easy as sending a message. The customer is not required to give bank account details for the fund transfer through the UPI payment system.

Unique Identification (UID) System: UID system has been introduced in India with biometrics to establish proof of identity of residents in India. It is an important step towards ensuring that residents in India can access the resources and benefits they are entitled to.

Unstructured Supplementary Service Data (USSD): *99# Banking: Mobile banking has brought the bank account in your hand. Today, you can check bank-balance, get a mini statement and transfer fund through the mobile banking. But, what if you do not have a smart phone or you do not have the internet? The answer to this problem is the USSD based mobile banking. Just dial *99# and you can do all those things which are available to a person with smart phone and 3G data. Almost every bank supports *99# USSD mobile banking service. The code which directly communicates with the server of a telecom company is called as the USSD. This code starts with * (asterisk) and ends with # (hash). A special number *99# is fixed to access the banking services. This number works across the banks. This system of banking transaction is termed as the National Unified USSD Platform (NUUP).

Virtual Currency: According to the European Central Bank, virtual currency is a digital representation of value, not issued by a central bank, credit institution or e-money institution, which, in some circumstances, can be used as an alternative to money.

Wireless Fidelity (Wi-Fi): It refers to certain types of wireless local area network (WLAN) used across the world. Wi-fi networks can be of two types, the open type where anyone can have access or the closed type requiring passwords.

1

Demonetization of High Denomination Currency Notes in India

"Our generation did not get the opportunity of fighting for the freedom of our nation but today we have the historic opportunity to weed out the menace of corruption and black money to secure the future of our nation".

Prime Minister Shri Narendra Modi

1.1 Demonetization Defined

Demonetization is the act of stripping a currency unit of its status as legal tender. [1] Demonetization is necessary whenever there is a change of national currency. The old unit of currency must be retired and replaced with a new currency unit. The process of demonetization involves either introducing new notes or coins of the same currency or completely replacing the old currency with new currency. The opposite of demonetization is remonetization where a form of payment is restored as legal tender. There are multiple reasons why nations demonetize their local units of currency. Some reasons include combating inflation, curbing corruption, and discouraging a cash system.

1.2 History and Background

Historically, previous Indian governments had demonetised bank notes. In January 1946, banknotes of ₹ 1,000 and ₹ 10,000 were withdrawn and new notes of ₹ 1,000, ₹ 5,000 and ₹ 10,000 were introduced in 1954. The Janata Party coalition government had again demonetised banknotes of ₹ 1,000, ₹ 5,000 and ₹ 10,000 on January 16, 1978 as a means of curbing counterfeit money and black money.

In 2012, the Central Board of Direct Taxes had recommended against demonetization, saying in a report that "demonetization may not be a solution for tackling black money in the economy, which is largely held in the form of *benami* properties, bullion and jewellery". According to data from income tax probes, black money holders keep only 6 percent or less of their ill-gotten wealth as cash, hence targeting this cash may not be a successful strategy.

In terms of value, the annual report of the Reserve Bank of India (RBI) of March 31, 2016 stated that total bank notes in circulation valued to ₹ 16.42 trillion of which nearly 86 percent (around ₹ 14.18 trillion) were ₹ 500 and ₹ 1,000 banknotes.

Prior to the announcement, Prime Minister Modi had, time and again, reiterated his commitment to eradicate the menace of black money. The very first decision of the Prime Minister-led NDA government was the formation of a SIT on black money. A law was passed in 2015 on disclosure of foreign bank accounts.

In August 2016, strict rules were put in place to curtail *benami* transactions. During the same period, a scheme to declare black money was introduced. Prime Minister raised the issue of black money at the global forums, including multilateral summits and bilateral meetings with the world leaders.

The Government of India devised an Income Declaration Scheme (IDS), which opened on June 1, 2016 and ended on September 30, 2016. Under the scheme, the black money holders could come clean by declaring the assets, paying the tax and a penalty of 45 percent thereafter.

Various policies and programmes announced by the Prime Minister, from time to time, have led to India emerging as a bright spot in the global economy. India is a preferred destination for investment and India is also an easier place to do business in. Leading financial agencies have shared their optimism about India's growth as well. Combined with this, Indian enterprise and innovation has received a fillip due to the *Make-in-India*, *Start-up India* and *Stand-up India* initiatives that seek to encourage enterprise, innovation and research in India. However, the problems of black money and corruption have been plaguing the economy.

1.3 Prime Minister's Historic Announcement to Withdraw Legal Tender Character of ₹ 500 and ₹ 1000 Notes

In a historical move to fight against the evils of black money, corruption, money laundering, financing of terrorists and counterfeit notes, the Government of India decided to withdraw the legal tender character of ₹ 500 and ₹ 1,000 banknotes of the Mahatma Gandhi Series from the midnight of November 8, 2016. The announcement was made by no less a person than the Prime Minister Shri Narendra Modi himself in an unscheduled live televised address to the nation on the evening of November 8, 2016.

The demonetized banknotes accounted for 86 percent of the country's cash supply.

Government also announced the issuance of new ₹ 500 and ₹ 2,000 banknotes of the Mahatma Gandhi New Series in exchange for the old banknotes. Banknotes of ₹ 100, ₹ 50, ₹ 20, ₹ 10, ₹ 5, ₹ 2 and ₹ 1 remained as legal tenders and thus unaffected by the decision of the Government.

Persons holding old notes of ₹ 500 or ₹ 1,000 could deposit these notes in bank or post offices from November 10, 2016 onwards till December 30, 2016. There were also some limits placed on the withdrawals of new notes from ATMs and banks.

The Government's move was aimed at eradicating counterfeit currency, fighting tax evasion, eliminating black money, curbing terrorist financing and promoting a cashless economy.

Prime Minister assured the people that these decisions would fully protect the interests of honest and hard-working citizens of India and that those ₹ 500 and ₹ 1,000 notes hoarded by anti-national and anti-social elements would become worthless pieces of paper. He reiterated that the steps taken by the Government would strengthen the hands of the common citizens in the fight against corruption, black money and counterfeit notes.

Fully sensitive to some of the difficulties the common citizens may face in the coming days, the Prime Minister announced a series of steps to help overcome the potential problems. He stated that on humanitarian grounds, ₹ 500 and ₹ 1,000 notes would be accepted at government hospitals, pharmacies in government hospitals (with prescription of a doctor), booking counters for railway tickets, government buses, airline ticket counters, petrol, diesel and gas stations of oil companies of public sector undertakings (PSUs), consumer co-operative stores authorized by the Central or State Government, milk booths authorized by State Governments, and crematoria and burial grounds.

He emphasized that there was no restriction on any kind of non-cash payments by cheques, demand drafts, debit or credit cards and electronic funds transfer.

In his address, the Prime Minister shared the insight into how the magnitude of cash in circulation was linked to inflation and how the inflation situation has worsened due to the cash deployed through corrupt means. He added that it adversely affected the poor and the neo-middle class people. He cited the example of the problems being faced by the honest citizens while buying houses.

By making the high denomination notes worthless, individuals and entities with huge sums of black money were forced to convert the money at a bank which is by law required to acquire tax information from the entity. If the entity could not provide proof of making any tax payments on the cash, a tax penalty of 200 percent of the tax owed was imposed.

After the official announcement by Prime Minister Modi, the Governor of the Reserve Bank of India, Urjit Patel, and Economic Affairs secretary, Shaktikanta Das explained at a press conference that while the supply of notes of all denominations had increased by 40 percent between 2011 and 2016, the ₹ 500 and ₹ 1,000 banknotes increased by 76 percent and 109 percent respectively during this period, owing to forgery. This forged cash was then used to fund terrorist activities against India. As a result, the decision to eliminate the notes had been taken.

Patel also informed that the decision had been made about six months ago, and the printing of new banknotes of denomination ₹ 500 and ₹ 2,000 had already started. However, only the top members of the government, security agencies and the central bank were aware of the move.

1.4 Objectives of the Scheme: These were as under:

1.4.1 Eliminating Black Money: In recent years, the issue of corruption and black money has come to the forefront after a series of financial scandals. Generation of black money—and its stashing abroad in tax havens and offshore financial centres—has dominated discussions and debates in public fora during the recent past. Members of the Parliament, the Supreme Court of India and the public at large have unequivocally expressed concern on the issue, particularly after some reports suggested enormous estimates of such unaccounted wealth being held abroad.

After uproar in the Parliament, the Government of India came out with a *White Paper* on Black Money in May 2012. The *White Paper* presented the different facets of black money and its complex relationship with policy and administrative regime in the country. It also reflected upon the policy options and strategies that the Government had been pursuing to address the issue of black money and corruption in public life.

To meet the deadline set by the Honourable Supreme Court for the previous Government, the new Government of Prime Minister Narendra Modi constituted a Special Investigation Team (SIT), soon after assuming office on May 26, 2014. Headed by Justice M.B. Shah, a former judge of the Supreme Court, SIT was notified on May 27, 2014 to look into the issue of black money.

1.4.2 Curbing Corruption: Corruption is both morally abhorrent and imposes economic costs. Corruption distorts the decision-making mechanism and leads to an inefficient distribution of resources. Improving anti-corruption efforts is one of the highest rated priorities of the Government of India.

1.4.3 Preventing Money Laundering: *Money laundering* is the process of transforming the proceeds of crime and corruption into ostensibly legitimate assets. In recent years, prevention of money laundering has assumed importance in international financial relationships. [2]

1.4.4 Eradicating Counterfeit Currency: The incidence of fake Indian currency notes in higher denomination had increased. For ordinary persons, the fake notes looked similar to genuine notes, even though no security feature had been copied. The fake notes were used for anti-national and illegal activities. High denomination notes had been misused by terrorists and for hoarding black money. In the cash-based economy of India, circulation of fake Indian currency notes was a menace.

1.4.5 Fighting Tax Evasion: Black money and tax evasion have been eating into the social and moral fabric of the Indian society. They are undermining the socio-economic objectives of national policies. They are responsible for conspicuous and wasteful consumption, reduced savings, and increasing gap between the rich and the poor. Black money in social, economic and political space of the country has a debilitating effect on the institutions of governance and conduct of public policy in the country. Governance failure adversely affects the interests of vulnerable and disadvantaged sections of the society. The success of an inclusive growth strategy critically hinges on the capacity of society to root out the evil of corruption and black money from its very foundations.

The effects of tax evasion, resulting in black money, on an economy are indeed disastrous. Tax evasion leads to the creation of black money which in turn is a menace to the economy in its own way. Tax evasion and black money encourage concentration of economic power in the hands of undesirable groups in the country.

1.4.6 Combating Terrorist Financing: India has been a victim of terrorist attacks time and again. Demonetization scheme is expected to choke funding for arms smuggling, espionage, and terrorism through *hawala* transactions. [3]

1.4.7 Promoting a Cashless Economy: The benefits of a cashless economy include: (a) reduced cash and hence more safety, (b) faster payment, (c) reduced number of visits to banks,

(d) interest earning on money in the bank, (e) quick settlement of transactions, and (f) improved accounting and book keeping.

In order to promote the above objectives, the scheme to withdraw legal tender character of old bank notes in the denominations of ₹ 500 and ₹ 1,000 was introduced.

1.5 Main Features of the Demonetization Scheme

1.5.1 Deposit of Demonetized Bank Notes: Demonetized notes could be deposited in banks and post offices from November 10, 2016 to December 30, 2016 without any limit.

1.5.2 Exchange of Demonetized Bank Notes: The legal tender character of the demonetized notes was withdrawn, they could not be used for transacting business and/or store of value for future usage. Demonetized notes could be exchanged for value at any of the 19 offices of the Reserve Bank of India and deposited at any of the bank branches of commercial banks/regional rural banks/co-operative banks (only urban co-operative banks and state co-operative Banks) or at any head post office or sub-post office.

1.5.3 Cash in Exchange for Demonetized Notes over the Bank Counter: From November 10, 2016 to November 24, 2016, over the counter exchange (in cash) of demonetized notes was permitted up to prescribed limits. However, the facility was withdrawn from November 25, 2016 in view of its misuse by unscrupulous elements.

1.5.4 Withdrawal of Cash against Cheque: Depositors were allowed to withdraw cash against withdrawal slip or cheque subject to a weekly limit of ₹ 24,000 (including withdrawals from ATMs) from their bank accounts.

Business entities having current accounts which were operational for the last 3 months or more were allowed to withdraw ₹ 50,000 per week. This could be done in a single transaction or multiple transactions.

1.5.5 Withdrawal from ATMs: The ATMs were progressively recalibrated. As and when they were recalibrated, the cash limit of such ATMs was ₹ 2,500 per day. This enabled dispensing of lower denomination currency notes for about ₹ 500 per withdrawal. Other ATMs which were yet to be recalibrated, continued to dispense ₹ 2,000 till they were recalibrated.

1.5.6 Withdrawal Limits for Farmers: Farmers were allowed to draw up to ₹ 25,000 per week in cash from their loan (including Kisan Credit Card limit) or deposit accounts subject to their accounts being compliant with the extant KYC norms. Demonetized bank notes could be used for making payments towards purchase of seeds from the centres, units or outlets belonging to the Central or State Governments, public sector undertakings, National or State Seeds Corporations, Central or State Agricultural Universities and the Indian Council of Agricultural Research, on production of proof of identity.

Rules regarding deposits and withdrawals were changed frequently depending upon the feedback received from the banking system.

1.6 Package for Promotion of Digital and Cashless Economy

In the aftermath of the cancellation of the legal tender character of old ₹ 500 and ₹ 1,000 notes, there has been a surge in the digital transactions through the use of credit/debit cards and mobile phone applications/e-wallets etc. To further accelerate this process, the Central Government announced on December 8, 2016, a package of incentives and measures for promotion of digital and cashless economy in the country. These incentives/measures are following:

1. The Central Government petroleum PSUs (public sector undertakings) shall give incentive by offering a discount at the rate of 0.75 percent of the sale price to consumers on purchase of petrol/diesel if payment is made through digital means. Nearly 4.5 crore customers buy petrol or diesel at such petrol pumps per day who can take benefit of this incentive scheme. It is estimated that petrol/diesel worth ₹ 1,800 crore is sold per day to the customers out of which nearly 20 percent was being paid through digital means. In the month of November 2016, it increased to 40

percent and the cash transaction of ₹ 360 crore per day got shifted to cashless transaction methods. The incentive scheme has the potential of shifting at least 30 percent more customers to digital means which will further reduce the cash requirement of nearly ₹ 2 lakh crore per year at the petrol pumps.

2. To expand digital payment infrastructure in rural areas, the Central Government through NABARD will extend financial support to eligible banks for deployment of 2 PoS devices each in 1 lakh villages with a population of less than 10,000. These PoS machines are intended to be deployed at primary co-operative societies, milk societies, agricultural input dealers to facilitate agri-related transactions through digital means. This will benefit farmers of 1 lakh village covering a total population of nearly 75 crore who will have the facility to transact cashless in their villages for their agri needs.

3. The Central Government through NABARD will also support rural regional banks and co-operative banks to issue "Rupay Kisan Cards" to 4.32 crore Kisan Credit Card holders to enable them to make digital transactions at PoS machines/micro ATMs/ATMs.

4. Railway, through its sub-urban railway network, shall provide incentive by way of discount up to 0.5 percent to customers for monthly or seasonal tickets from January 1, 2017, if payment is made through digital means. Nearly 80 lakh passengers use seasonal or monthly ticket on suburban railways, largely in cash, spending nearly ₹ 2,000 crore per year. As more and more passengers will shift to digital means, the cash requirement may get reduced by ₹ 1,000 crore per year in near future.

5. All railway passengers buying online ticket shall be given free accidental insurance cover of up to ₹ 10 lakh. Nearly 14 lakh railway passengers are buying tickets everyday out of which 58 percent tickets are bought online through digital means. It is expected that another 20 percent passengers may shift to digital payment methods of buying

railway tickets. Hence, nearly 11 lakh passengers per day will be covered under the accidental insurance scheme.

6. For paid services, e.g. catering, accommodation, retiring rooms etc. being offered by the railways through its affiliated entities/corporations to the passengers, it will provide a discount of 5 percent for payment of these services through digital means. All the passengers travelling on railways availing these services may avail the benefit.

7. Public sector insurance companies will provide incentive, by way of discount or credit, up to 10 percent of the premium in general insurance policies and 8 percent in new life policies of Life Insurance Corporation sold through the customer portals, in case payment is made through digital means.

8. The Central Government departments and PSUs will ensure that transactions fee/MDR charges associated with payment through digital means shall not be passed on to the consumers and all such expenses shall be borne by them. State Governments have been advised that the State Governments and its organizations should also consider absorbing the transaction fee/MDR charges related to digital payments to them and consumers should not be asked to bear it.

9. Public sector banks are advised that merchant should not be required to pay more than ₹ 100 per month as monthly rental for PoS terminals/micro ATMs/mobile PoS from the merchants to bring small merchants on board the digital payment eco-system. Nearly 6.5 lakh machines by public sector banks have been issued to merchants who will be benefited by the lower rentals while promoting digital transactions. With lower rentals, more merchants will install such machines and promote digital transactions.

10. No service tax will be charged on digital transaction charges/MDR for transactions up to ₹ 2,000 per transaction.

11. For the payment of toll at toll plazas on national highways using RFID card/fast tags, a discount of 10 percent will be available to users during the year 2016-17.

1.7 Reactions to Demonetization

The government claimed that the demonetization was an effort to stop counterfeiting of the current banknotes allegedly used for funding terrorism, as well as a crack down on black money in the country. The move was also described as an effort to reduce corruption, use of drugs, and smuggling.

However, in the days following the demonetization, banks and ATMs across the country faced severe cash shortages affecting small businesses, agriculture sector, and the transportation sector. People seeking to exchange their notes had to stand in queues due to the rush to exchange cash.

The move received support from several bankers as well as from some international commentators. However, it was heavily criticized by members of the opposition parties, leading to debates in both houses of the Parliament and triggering organized protests against the government at several places across India. The Government opined that the queues due to demonetization were the last queues that would end all other queues.

Analysts were unanimous in holding the view that the demonetization move of the Government would hit the economy hard in the short-term albeit benefitting the country in the long-run. However, the demonetization move was expected to have a negative impact on inflation. Consumers were refraining from making any purchases except essential items from the consumer staples, healthcare, and energy segments. Activity in the real estate sector, which includes a lot of cash and undocumented transactions, slowed down significantly.

1.8 Pradhan Mantri Garib Kalyan Deposit Scheme, 2016

Prime Minister Shri Narendra Modi is trying his level best to eliminate the black money from the Indian economy. Those who have not declared their unaccounted money were given the last chance through this scheme.

This scheme was announced by the Government of India on December 16, 2016. It came into force from December 17, 2016 and shall be valid till March 31, 2017.

The salient features of the Scheme are as under:

- Declaration under the Scheme can be made by any person in respect of undisclosed income in the form of cash or deposits in an account with bank or post office or specified entity.

- Tax at the rate of 30 percent of the undisclosed income, surcharge at the rate of 33 percent of tax and penalty at the rate of 10 percent of such income is payable besides mandatory deposit of 25 percent of the undisclosed income in Pradhan Mantri Garib Kalyan Deposit Scheme, 2016. The deposits are interest free and have a lock-in period of 4 years.

- The income declared under the Scheme shall not be included in the total income of the declarant under the Income-tax Act for any assessment year.

Non-declaration of undisclosed cash or deposit in accounts under the Scheme will render such undisclosed income liable to tax, surcharge and cess totalling to 77.25 percent of such income, if declared in the return of income. In case the same is not shown in the return of income, a further penalty at the rate of 10 percent of tax shall also be levied followed by prosecution. It may be noted that the provisions for levy of penalty for misreporting of income at the rate of 200 percent of tax payable under Section 270A of the Income-tax Act have not been amended and shall continue to apply with respect to cases falling under the said section.

The Taxation Laws (Second Amendment) Act, 2016 has also amended the penalty provisions in respect of search and seizure cases. The existing slab for penalty of 10 percent, 20 percent and 60 percent of income levied under Section 271AAB has been rationalised to 30 percent of income, if the income is admitted and taxes are paid. Otherwise, a penalty at the rate of 60 percent of income shall be levied.

Endnotes

1. Legal tender is any official medium of payment recognized by law that can be used to extinguish a public or private debt, or meet a financial obligation. National currency is legal tender in practically every country. A creditor is obligated to accept legal

tender toward repayment of a debt. Legal tender can only be issued by the national body that is authorized to do so, such as the RBI in the case of India. Widely accepted currencies such as the US dollar and Euro are accepted as legal tender in many nations, especially those where foreign currencies are in short supply. Countries with extensive business and cultural ties may also accept each other's currencies as legal tender in limited amounts.

2. Prevention of Money Laundering Act (PMLA), 2002 was enacted to prevent money laundering and provide for confiscation of property derived from, or involved in, money laundering and for matters connected therewith or incidental thereto. The Act also addresses international obligations under the Political Declaration and Global Programme of Action adopted by the General Assembly of the United Nations to prevent money laundering. For details of Prevention of Money Laundering Act (PMLA), 2002 and Reserve Bank of India's Guidelines on money laundering, see section 3.5.1 of chapter 3 of this book.

3. **Hawala Transactions:** The hawala system has existed since the 8th century between Arabic and Muslim traders alongside the Silk Road and beyond as a protection against theft. It is believed to have arisen in the financing of long-distance trade around the emerging capital trade centers in the early medieval period.

   Meaning: Hawala (reference/trust) is a popular and informal value transfer system based on the past record and honour of a huge network of money brokers—primarily located in the Middle East and the Indian subcontinent—operating outside of, or parallel to, traditional banking, financial channels, and remittance systems. Dubai has been standing out for decades as a welcoming hub for hawala transactions worldwide.

   Working Mechanism: In the most basic variant of the hawala system, money is transferred via a network of hawala brokers. It is the transfer of money without actually moving it or money transfer without money movement.

   Let us suppose a customer (named A) approaches a hawala broker (named B) in New York and gives a sum of money (US$ 1,000) that is to be transferred to a recipient (named C) in New Delhi. Along with the money, A specifies something like a password (e.g.

red rose) that will lead to the money being paid out. The hawala broker B calls another hawala broker (named D) in New Delhi—the recipient's city—and informs D about the agreed password and other details regarding funds and meeting place and time. Now, the intended recipient (C)—who also has been informed by A about the password etc. approaches D and tells him the agreed password. If the password is correct, then D releases the transferred sum to C in Indian rupees (₹ 70,000 if 1 US$ = ₹ 70), usually minus a small commission. B now basically owes D the money that D had paid out to C. Thus, D has to trust B's promise to settle the debt at a later date.

Apparently, hawala mechanism can work in the reverse also if funds are to be transferred from New Delhi to New York.

Features: The unique feature of the system is that no promissory instruments are exchanged between the hawala brokers. The transaction takes place entirely on the trust/honour system. As the system does not depend on the legal enforceability of claims, it can operate even in the absence of a legal and juridical environment. Trust and extensive use of connections, such as family relations and regional affiliations, are the components that distinguish it from other remittance systems.

Informal records are kept of individual transactions, and a running tally of the amount owed by one broker to another is kept. Settlements of debts between hawala brokers can take a variety of forms (such as goods, services, properties etc.) and need not take the form of direct cash transactions.

In addition to commissions, hawala brokers often earn their profits through bypassing official exchange rates. Generally, the funds enter the system in the source country's currency (in this example, US$) and leave the system in the recipient country's currency (in this example, Indian rupees). As settlements often take place without any foreign exchange transactions, they can be made at other than official exchange rates.

Hawala is attractive to customers because it provides a fast and convenient transfer of funds, usually with a far lower commission than that charged by banks. Its advantages are most pronounced when the receiving country applies unprofitable exchange rate regulations or when the banking system in the receiving country is less efficient. Hawala is often used for migrant workers' remittances to their countries of origin.

Hawala route can be used to facilitate drug smuggling, money laundering, tax evasion, and anonymously movement of fund for terrorist activities. Hence, it is illegal in many countries including India.

2

The Menace of Black Money in India

Black money and tax evasion are eating into the social and moral fabric of Indian society. They are responsible for conspicuous and wasteful consumption, reduced savings, and increasing gap between the rich and the poor. Black money in social, economic and political space of the country has a debilitating effect on the institutions of governance and conduct of public policy in the country. Governance failure adversely affects the interests of vulnerable and disadvantaged sections of society. The success of an inclusive growth strategy critically hinges on the capacity of society to root out the evil of corruption and black money from its very foundations.

In recent years, the issue of corruption and black money has come in the forefront after a series of financial scandals. Generation of black money—and its stashing abroad in tax havens and offshore financial centres—has dominated discussions and debate in public fora during the recent past. Members of Parliament, the Supreme Court of India and the public at large have unequivocally expressed concern on the issue, particularly after some reports suggested enormous estimates of such unaccounted wealth being held abroad.

After uproar in Parliament, Government of India came out with a *White Paper* on Black Money in May 2012. The *White Paper* presented the different facets of black money and its complex relationship with policy and administrative regime in the country. It also reflected upon the policy options and strategies that the Government had been pursuing to address the issue of black money and corruption in public life.

To meet the deadline set by the Honourable Supreme Court for the previous Government, the New Government of Prime Minister Narendra Modi constituted a Special Investigation Team

(SIT), soon after assuming office on May 26, 2014. Headed by Justice M.B. Shah, a former judge of the Supreme Court, SIT was notified on May 27, 2014 to look into the issue of black money.

SIT, as ordered by the Court, will include the revenue secretary, directors of the Central Bureau of Investigation (CBI), Intelligence Bureau (IB), Research and Analysis Wing (RAW), Enforcement Directorate (ED), Chairman of the Central Board of Direct Taxes (CBDT), and a Deputy Governor of the Reserve Bank of India (RBI).

SIT has been charged with the responsibility and duties of investigation, initiation of proceedings and prosecution in some high-profile tax evasion cases. The panel will have jurisdiction in cases where investigations have commenced, are pending or awaiting to be initiated or have been completed.

Terms of reference for the SIT require it to investigate "with respect to unaccounted monies being stashed in foreign banks by Indians or other entities operating in India that may arise in the course of such investigations and proceedings".

SIT will prepare a comprehensive action plan, including creation of an institutional structure that could enable the country to fight the battle against unaccounted money.

It may be recalled that on May 1, 2014 the Central Government had reported to the Supreme Court that investigations had been concluded against 18 of the 26 individuals that had bank accounts in Liechtenstein. It also said that these names were received from Germany and investigation had concluded in 17 cases of which no evidence was found against 8 and the investigation were concluded against them.

2.1 Black Money Defined

There is no uniform and universally acceptable definition of black money in fiscal literature. Generally speaking, the term *black money* stands for money earned by illegal means and kept secret and unaccounted for. It is widely used for smuggling activities, hoarding of scarce commodities (for the purpose of speculation, profiteering, and black marketing), bribing government officials, financing political activities, and ostentatious living. Secret business deals through black money in turn lead to tax evasion and a vicious circle is created in which one evil thrives on the other.

The term *black money* has many synonyms including *underground economy, parallel economy, shadow economy unofficial economy, and unaccounted economy*. All these terms usually refer to any income on which the taxes imposed by government or public authorities have not been paid. Thus, *black money* can be defined as assets or resources that have neither been reported to the public authorities at the time of their generation nor disclosed at any point of time during their possession.

In addition to wealth earned through illegal means, the term black money would also include legal income that is concealed from public authorities: (a) to evade payment of taxes (income tax, excise duty, sales tax, stamp duty etc), (b) to evade payment of other statutory contributions, (c) to evade compliance with the provisions of industrial laws, and/or to evade compliance with other laws and administrative procedures.

Black money may be generated in two ways. Firstly, money may be generated through illegitimate activities not permissible under the law—like drug trade, terrorism, and corruption—and which are punishable under the legal framework of the state. Secondly, money may be generated and accumulated by failing to pay the dues to the public exchequer in one form or the other. In this case, the activities undertaken by the perpetrator could be legitimate and otherwise permissible under the law of the land but he fails to report the income so generated, comply with the tax requirements, or pay the dues to the public exchequer, leading to the generation of unaccounted wealth.

The comparison of the above two ways in which black money is generated is important to understand the problems and adopt appropriate policy measures to curb and control black money. It is clear that the first category is one where an iron fist is required on the part of government and its various law enforcing agencies. However, it is the second category where the issue becomes far more complex and may require new legislations/modification of existing laws and reforms in current policies and strategies to promote compliance with laws (particularly tax laws), regulations, and rules. The revamped institutional structure should also discourage the active economic agents of society from generating, hoarding, and illicitly transferring abroad such unaccounted wealth.

2.2 Global Concerns against Black Money/Tax Evasion

The global economic conditions deteriorated sharply during the year 2008 with several advanced economies experiencing their sharpest declines in the post-Second World War period. The associated adverse shocks spreading across developing countries accentuated the synchronised global slowdown. The global financial environment entered a crisis phase following the growing distress among large international financial institutions and the declaration of bankruptcy of Lehman Brothers.

The financial crisis of 2008 and the resultant need for protecting revenues further strengthened the need for coordinated global efforts to tackle the challenges posed by tax haven-mediated arrangements for evading tax.

2.2.1 United Nations Convention against Illicit Traffic in Narcotic Drugs and Psychotropic Substances: The purpose of this Convention is to promote cooperation among the parties so that they may more effectively address the various aspects of illicit traffic in narcotic drugs and psychotropic substances having an international dimension. The Convention also calls for criminalisation of money laundering, the freezing, seizure and confiscation of the proceeds of crime, and international cooperation. India joined this Convention on March 27, 1990.

2.2.2 Multilateral Convention on Mutual Administrative Assistance in Tax Matters: This Convention was developed jointly by the Council of Europe and the Organization for Economic Development and Co-operation (OECD) [8] and was opened for signature by the member states of both organizations on January 25, 1998. This multilateral instrument, which was initially signed by 15 countries, provides for all possible forms of administrative cooperation between states in the assessment and collection of taxes, in particular with a view to combating tax avoidance and evasion.

In response to the April 2009 call by the G20 [9] for a global instrument to fight international tax evasion and avoidance, the Convention has been brought up to the internationally agreed standard on information exchange for tax purposes, in particular by requiring the exchange of bank information on request through an amending Protocol, which entered into force on June 1, 2011. The amended Protocol also provides for the opening of the Convention to all countries. India signed the Convention on January 26, 2012 and ratified it on February 2, 2012, thus becoming the first country outside the OECD and European countries to join it. There are at present 33 signatories to the Convention and 13 of them have ratified it.

This Convention provides many advantages. As more countries sign it, the task of information exchange will get increasingly facilitated. It is likely to be an important instrument for cooperation in the area of assistance in tax collection. A unique feature of this convention is the facility for serving of notices issued by one tax administration through another tax administration.

2.2.3 United Nations Convention against Corruption: On May 9, 2011, India became the 152nd country to ratify this Convention which was signed on December 9, 2005. The objectives of this Convention are as under:

1. To promote and strengthen measures for preventing and combating corruption more efficiently and effectively.
2. To promote, facilitate, and support international cooperation and technical assistance in the prevention of and fight against corruption including in asset recovery.
3. To promote integrity, accountability measures, and the criminalisation of the most prevalent forms of corruption in both public and private sectors.

The Convention requires the state parties to criminalise bribery of national public officials, foreign public officials and officials of public international organizations, embezzlement, misappropriation or other divisions of property by a public official, laundering of proceeds of crime, obstruction of justice, and illicit enrichment.

Under the Convention, countries should have mechanisms for freezing, seizure, and confiscation of the proceeds of crime and cooperate in criminal matters by extradition and mutual legal assistance to the greatest possible extent. The return of assets is a fundamental objective of this Convention and countries are to afford one another the widest measure of cooperation and assistance in this regard. It prescribes mechanisms for recovery of property through international cooperation for purposes of confiscation.

2.2.4 United Nations Convention against Transnational Organized Crime (Palermo Convention): On May 5, 2011, India ratified this Convention which was signed on December 12, 2002. The purpose of this Convention is to promote international cooperation in preventing and combating transnational organized crime more effectively. Under the Convention, countries are to take measures against smuggling of migrants by land, sea, and air as well as manufacturing and trafficking of firearms and ammunition. The Convention will help India get international cooperation in tracing, seizure, freezing, and confiscation of the proceeds of crimes under a wide range of mutual legal assistance clauses, even with countries with which it has no mutual legal assistance treaties.

2.2.5 International Convention for the Suppression of the Financing of Terrorism: India signed this Convention on September 8, 2000 and ratified it on April 22, 2003. It requires each state party to take appropriate measures, in accordance with its domestic legal principles, for the detection and freezing, seizure, or forfeiture of any funds used or allocated for the purposes of committing the offences described, as well as take alleged offenders into custody, prosecute or extradite them, cooperate in preventive measures and countermeasures, and exchange information and evidence needed in related criminal proceedings. The offences referred to in the Convention are deemed to be extraditable offences between state parties under existing extradition treaties and under the Convention itself.

2.2.6 Financial Action Task Force (FATF): It is an inter-governmental body established in 1989 by the Ministers of its Member jurisdictions. The objectives of the FATF are to set standards and promote effective implementation of legal, regulatory and operational measures for combating money laundering, terrorist financing and other related threats to the integrity of the international financial system. The FATF is therefore a *policy-making body* which works to generate the necessary political will to bring about national legislative and regulatory reforms in these areas.

The FATF has developed a series of Recommendations that are recognised as the international standard for combating of money laundering and the financing of terrorism and proliferation of weapons of mass destruction. They form the basis for a co-ordinated response to these threats to the integrity of the financial system and help ensure a level playing field. First issued in 1990, the FATF Recommendations were revised in 1996, 2001, 2003 and most recently in 2012 to ensure that they remain up to date and relevant, and they are intended to be of universal application.

The FATF monitors the progress of its members in implementing necessary measures, reviews money laundering and terrorist financing techniques and counter-measures, and promotes the adoption and implementation of appropriate measures globally. In collaboration with other international stakeholders, the FATF works to identify national-level vulnerabilities with the aim of protecting the international financial system from misuse.

The FATF's decision-making body, the FATF Plenary, meets three times per year.

2.2.7 Asia/Pacific Group on Money Laundering (APG): It is an international organisation (regionally focused) consisting of 41 members and a number of international and regional observers including the United Nations, IMF, FATF, Asian Development Bank, ASEAN Secretariat, Pacific Islands Forum Secretariat and World Bank.

APG is closely affiliated with the Financial Action Task Force (FATF), whose Secretariat is located in the OECD headquarters in Paris, France. All APG members commit to effectively implement the FATF's international standards for anti-money laundering, combating the financing of terrorism and the financing of proliferation, referred to as the 40 Recommendations. The 40 Recommendations were revised and adopted by the FATF membership after world-wide consultation (including the private sector) in February 2012. Part of this commitment includes implementing targeted financial sanctions against terrorism and the financing of the proliferation of weapons of mass destruction (WMD).

2.3 Sectors/Activities More Prone to Black Money Generation

The source of generation of black money can lie in any sphere of economic activity. Nevertheless, there are certain sectors and activities which are more prone to black money generation. These include, *inter alia*, the following:

1. Land and real estate transactions.
2. Bullion and jewellery dealings.
3. Complex financial market transactions (derivatives).
4. Charitable (non-profit) activities.
5. Informal sector and cash economy.
6. Self-employed professionals.
7. External trade and transfer pricing.

2.3.1 Land and Real Estate Transactions: Due to rising prices of real estate, the high tax incidence applicable on real estate transactions in the form of stamp duty and capital gains tax can create incentives for tax evasion through under-reporting of transaction price. This can lead to both generation and investment of black money. The buyer has the option of investing his black money by paying cash in addition to the documented sale consideration. This also leads to generation of black money in the hands of the recipient. [1]

2.3.2 Bullion and Jewellery Dealings: Cash sales in the gold and jewellery trade are quite common and serve two purposes. The purchase allows the buyer the option of converting black money into gold and bullion, while it gives the trader the option of keeping his unaccounted wealth in the form of stock, not disclosed in the books or valued at less than market price.

2.3.3 Complex Financial Market Transactions: Financial market transactions can involve black money in different forms. Rigging of markets by the market operators is one such means. This may involve use of dummy companies, trading in derivatives [2], participatory notes (PNs) [3] and other forms of manipulated trading.

2.3.4 Charitable (Non-profit) Activities: Taxation laws allow certain privileges and incentives for promoting charitable (non-profit) activities. Misuse of such benefits and manipulations through entities claimed to be constituted for non-profit motive are among possible sources of generation of black money.

Generally, charitable trusts are not required to pay tax on donations received by them. Similarly, income tax laws allow charitable contributions as deductions from taxable income. Since marginal rates of tax are high at upper brackets of income, charitable contributions are less costly to wealthy people.

These provisions are sometimes misused in the sense that donors exercise considerable control in managing the affairs of trusts/institutions to which charitable contributions are made. Private or family interest in the management of charitable trusts leads to control in the use of what are essentially public funds. Family control over a charitable trust generally leads to promoting private interest, defeating in the process the essential purpose of the tax concession. To quote, "Charitable organisations, non-government organisations (NGOs), and associations receiving foreign contributions are required to file an annual return to the Ministry of Home Affairs in Form FC-3. In the said form, only the name and address of the foreign donors are mentioned, with no further details of the beneficial owners. It is possible that in many such cases, the black money generated by Indians is being routed back to India". [4]

2.3.5 Informal Sector and Cash Economy: In its Report on Definitional and Statistical Issues Relating to the Informal Economy, submitted in 2008, the National Commission for Enterprises in the Unorganized Sector (Chairman: Arjun Sengupta), defined unorganized (informal) sector as the "sector consisting of all unincorporated private enterprises owned by individuals or households engaged in the sale and production of goods and services operated on a proprietary or partnership basis and with less than ten total workers". [5]

The issue of black money is related to the magnitude of cash transactions in the informal economy. Factors like dependence on agriculture, existence of a large informal sector, and insufficient banking infrastructure with large un-banked and under-banked areas contribute to the large cash economy in India.

2.3.6 Self-employed Professionals: Although evasion of tax is a common tendency among people belonging to different groups, opportunities for it vary according to the nature of income earned by taxpayers. In the case of income from salaries and interest from deposits, evasion is less likely because of proper recording and auditing of transactions, and deduction of tax at source. However, opportunities for tax evasion are very large in the case of self-employed in business and professions. Doctors, lawyers, architects, property dealers, individual contractors, jewellers, caterers, event managers can evade taxes more easily than others. They can insist on their customers to pay them in cash or accept invoices which underestimate the payment.

Moreover, salaried persons envy tax evasion opportunities available to self-employed professionals and retail traders, and are tempted to conceal their incomes from non-salary sources.

2.3.7 External Trade and Transfer Pricing: Differing tax rates in different countries can create perverse incentives for corporations to shift taxable income from jurisdictions with relatively high tax rates to jurisdictions with relatively low tax rates as a means of minimising their tax liability. For example, a foreign parent company could use internal *transfer prices* for reducing its worldwide tax payment. In fact, transfer pricing [6] has emerged as the biggest tool for generation and transfer of black money.

2.4 Activities Leading to Generation of Black Money

2.4.1 Generation of Black Money through Illegal Activities: The *criminal component* of black money includes a host of illegal activities. Such activities—anti-social in nature—include, *inter alia*, the following:

1. Smuggling of goods.
2. Forgery, embezzlement, counterfeit currency, and other financial frauds (chit funds etc.).
3. Production/trade of contraband goods (e.g. narcotics, illicit liquor and arms).
4. Illegal mining and illegal felling of forests.
5. Hoarding and black marketing of price-controlled goods and services.
6. Theft, robbery, kidnapping and extortion, human trafficking, sexual exploitation and blackmailing.
7. Bribes to those holding public offices to secure favours: (a) altering land use, (b) regularizing authorized constructions, (c) speed money to circumvent/fast track procedures, and (d) commission to secure government purchase orders.

All above-mentioned activities are illegal and reflect declining social and moral values. These illegal activities are punishable under various Acts of the Central and State Governments which are administered by various law enforcement agencies. Effective implementation of these Acts is the responsibility of both the Central and State Governments. Some of these offences are included in the schedule of the Prevention of

Money Laundering Act, 2002.

2.4.2 Generation of Black Money through Legal Activities: Significant amount of black money, however, is generated through legally permissible economic activities. Though lawful, such activities are not disclosed/reported to the public authorities as per provisions of the law, thereby converting such income into black money. The failure to report/disclose such activities/income may be with the objective of evading taxes or avoiding the cost of compliance related to such reporting/disclosure under some other law.

Generally, a high burden of taxation provides a strong temptation to evade taxes. Sometimes the procedural regulations can be such that complying with them may increase the probability of further scrutiny and thereby the incidence of the burden of compliance. Such situations create incentive to conceal one's true state of affairs and thereby remain outside the reported and accounted proportion of one's activities.

With increased globalisation [7] and economic liberalisation, there has been a manifold increase in cross-border transactions. This has also resulted in increased opportunities for sophisticated devices to avoid tax payment using the different tax rules of different countries and use of tax havens. Global trade amongst various arms of multinational companies (MNCs) has also increased substantially and accounts for a significant proportion of global trade. It also means increasing misuse of transfer pricing, leading to estimations that developing countries might be losing significant resources due to transfer pricing manipulation.

One of the difficulties in preventing abuse of such transfer pricing arrangements is the large disparity between resources deployed by these multinationals and those available with tax administrators, particularly of developing countries. This requires enormous reforms for improving the capacity of tax administration and equipping it with the necessary resources to deal with such modern challenges.

2.5 Methods to Generate Black Money

Black money may be generated through the crude approach of not declaring or reporting the income or the activities leading to it. This is the likely approach in all cases of criminal, illegal, and impermissible activities. The same approach of not declaring or reporting activities and the income generated therefrom may also be followed in cases of failure to comply with regulatory obligations or tax evasion on income from legitimate activities. However, complete evasion or non-compliance may make such incomes vulnerable to detection by authorities and lead to adverse consequences for the generator.

As an alternative, a safer approach for generation of black money is often preferred, involving manipulation of financial records and accounting. Thus, the best way of classifying and understanding the various ways and means adopted by taxpayers for the generation of black money would be the *financial statement approach*. It elaborates different means by which the accounts prepared for reporting and presenting before the authorities are manipulated to misrepresent income, thereby generating income that amounts to black money.

As is well-known, any transaction entered into by the taxpayer must be reported in books of account which are summarized at the end of the year in the form of financial statements. The financial statements basically comprise: (a) statement of income and expenditure called *Profit and Loss Account* or *Income and Expenditure Account*, and (b) statement of assets and liabilities called *Balance Sheet*.

Different kinds of manipulations of financial statements resulting in tax evasion and the generation of black money are elaborated in the following paragraphs.

2.5.1 Out of Book Transactions: These include the following

A. No Books of Account: This is one of the simplest and most widely adopted methods of tax evasion and generation of black money. Transactions that may result in taxation of receipts or income are not entered in the books of account by the taxpayer. The taxpayer either does not maintain books of account or maintains two sets or records partial receipts only. This mode is generally prevalent among the micro and small enterprises and providers of unskilled and semi-skilled services.

B. Parallel Books of Accounts: This is a practice usually adopted by those who are obliged under the law, or due to business needs, to maintain books of account. In order to evade reporting activities or the income generated from them, they may resort to maintaining two sets of books of account—one for their own consumption with the objective of managing their business and the other one for the regulatory and tax authorities (income tax, excise, VAT). The second set of books of account, which is maintained for the purpose of satisfying the legal and regulatory obligations of reporting to different authorities, may be manipulated by omitting receipts or falsely inflating expenses, for the purpose of evading taxes or other regulatory requirements.

Other methods under this category include: (a) unaccounted assets, and (b) investments in shares of listed companies through dummy entities.

2.5.2 Manipulation of Books of Account: When books of accounts are required to be maintained by taxpayers under different laws (e.g. Income Tax Act, 1961, Companies Act, 1956) it may become difficult for these taxpayers to indulge in out of book transactions or to maintain parallel books of accounts. Such parties may resort to manipulation of the books of accounts to evade taxes.

A. Manipulation of Sales/Receipts: A taxpayer is required to pay taxes on profit or income which is the difference between sale proceeds or receipts and expenditure. Thus, manipulation of sales or receipts is the easiest method of tax evasion. Other innovative devices may include diversion of sales to associated enterprises, which may become more important if such enterprises are located in different tax jurisdictions and thereby may also give rise to issues related to international taxation and transfer pricing.

In the case of dummy associate entity, there can be a plethora of possible arrangements entered into by such entities to aid generation of black money. In its simplest form, the associate entity may not report its activities or income at all. The main entity may show sales to such a dummy associate entity at a lower price, thereby reducing its reported profits.

More complex scenarios can emerge if the dummy associate entity is situated in a low tax jurisdiction having very low tax rates. Thus, the profit of the Indian entity will be transferred to the low tax jurisdiction and money will be accumulated by the taxpayer in the books of accounts of the entity in the low tax jurisdiction.

Under-reporting of production is another means of artificially reducing tax liability. It may be resorted to for the purpose of evading central excise, sales tax, or income tax.

In short, the following means can be applied to manipulate sales/receipts: (a) suppression of sales/receipts, (b) diversion of sales to associated enterprises (dummy or genuine), (c) inter-relation between unaccounted sales and purchases, (d) artificial deferment of revenues, and (e) stamping of incorrect price.

B. Manipulation of Expenses: Since the income on which taxes are payable is arrived at after deducting the expenses of the business from the receipts, manipulation of expenses is a commonly adopted method of tax evasion. The expenses may be manipulated under different heads and result in under-reporting of income. It may involve inflation of expenses, sometimes by obtaining bogus or inflated invoices from the so called *bill masters*, who make bogus vouchers and charge nominal commission for this facility. Sometimes it can also involve *hawala* operators, who operate shell entities in the form of proprietorship firms, partnership firms, companies, and trusts. These operators may accept cheques for payments claimed as expense and return cash after charging some commission.

There have been instances of claims of bogus expenses to

foreign entities. The payments can be shown to foreign entities in the form of advertisement and marketing expenses or commission for purchases or sales. The funds may be remitted to the account of the foreign taxpayer and the money can either be withdrawn in cash or remitted back to India in the form of non-taxable receipts. Such money may also be accumulated in the form of unaccounted assets of the Indian taxpayer abroad.

Besides inflation of purchase/raw material cost, expenses like labour charges, entertainment expenses, and commission can be inflated or falsely booked to reduce profits.

C. Manipulation of Capital: The balance sheet of the taxpayer contains details of assets, liabilities, and capital. The capital of the taxpayer is the accumulated wealth which is invested in the form of assets or as working capital of the business. Manipulation of capital can be one of the ways of laundering black money and introducing it in the books of accounts. Manipulation of capital can take place, *inter alia*, through following means: (a) shares at high premium, (b) bogus gifts, and (c) bogus capital gains and purchase of bogus losses.

D. Manipulation of Closing Stock: Suppression of closing stock both in terms of quality and value is one of the most common methods of understating profit. Refiner versions of such practice may include omission of goods in transit paid for and debited to purchases, or omission of goods sent to the customer for approval. A more common approach is undervaluation of inventory (stock of unsold goods), which means that while the expenses are being accounted for in the books, the value being added is not accounted for, thereby artificially reducing the profits.

E. Manipulation of Capital Expenses: Over-invoicing plant and equipment or any capital asset is an approach adopted to claim higher depreciation and thereby reduce the profit of the business. Increase in capital can also be a means of enabling the businessman to borrow more funds from banks or raise capital from the market. It has been seen that such measures are sometimes resorted to at the time of bringing out a capital issue.

F. International Transactions through Associate Enterprises: Another way of manipulating accounted profits and taxes payable thereon may involve using associated enterprises in low tax jurisdictions through which goods or other material may be passed on to the concern. Inter-corporate transactions between these associate enterprises belonging to the same group or owned and controlled by the same set of parties may be arranged and manipulated in a way that leads to evasion of taxes. This can often be achieved by arrangements that shift taxable income to the low tax jurisdictions or tax havens, and may lead to accumulation of black money earned from within India to another country.

2.6 Consequences of Black Money/Tax Evasion

The nexus between tax evasion and black money and its distortion of the redistributive role of tax policy has been emphasized time and again. With a sizeable proportion of income and wealth evading taxation, the redistributive impact of progressive taxation is severely blunted. A reduction in the scale of black income generation would improve distribution of income and wealth after taxation. Besides, if the magnitude of tax evasion is significantly reduced, there would be a greater volume of tax revenue, and a greater volume of public expenditure benefiting the poorer section of the population would become possible.

Black money in social, economic and political space of the country has a debilitating effect on the institutions of governance and conduct of public policy in the country. Governance failure adversely affects the interests of vulnerable and disadvantaged sections of society. The success of an inclusive growth strategy critically depends on the capacity of society to root out the evil of corruption and black money from its very foundations. Undoubtedly, India needs a speedy transition towards a more transparent and result-oriented economic system.

The fight against generation and accumulation of black

money is far more complex and prolonged, requiring stronger intervention of the state. It needs a robust legal framework, commensurate administrative set up, and a very strong resolve to fight the menace.

2.7 Estimation of Black Money

Since black money is unaccounted for, there are no reliable estimates of it. Similarly, there is no well-defined and universally acceptable methodology for estimation of black money. Hence, all attempts at its estimation have produced results with wide variations. Several estimates have been floated—often without adequate factual basis—on the magnitude of black money generated in the country and the unaccounted wealth stashed aboard.

2.7.1 Estimation Techniques

A. Input-output Method [8]: It consists of using the input/output ratio along with the input to calculate the true output. It estimates black money as the difference between the declared output and the output expected on the basis of the input/output ratio. This method is deceptively simple and, though it may have some utility if applied to a uniform industry or a specific sector of the economy, it is unlikely to be of much help if applied to economy as a whole. It also ignores structural changes in the economy including those related to technology.

B. Money Circulation Approach: Another approach, adopted by the monetarists, is based on the fact that money is needed to circulate incomes in both the *black* and accounted for economies. As the official economy is known, the difference between that amount and the money in circulation could be assumed to be the circulating *black* component. An estimate of the velocity of money [9] enables an estimation of income circulated annually. A comparison of that with the income captured in the National Accounting System (NAS) gives the income which could be estimated as the black money in the economy. However, the assumption that the NAS represents accounted incomes accurately is not always true. Large proportions of income, such as those falling in the unorganized sector, are not accurately captured in NAS.

C. Survey Method: Under it, sample surveys are carried out for estimation of black money. These may be on the consumption pattern of a representative population sample, which is then compared to the total consumption of the country. In this method, the problems consist in getting a truly representative sample, and the willingness of persons in the sample size to reveal true facts. As is well-known, people are often unwilling to reveal their *true state of affairs* and admit any illegality before surveyors.

As regards black money stashed abroad, the White Paper on Black Money observed, "It is however useful to mention here one estimate of the amount of Indian deposits in Swiss banks (located in Switzerland) which has been made by the Swiss National Bank. Its spokesperson stated that at the end of 2010, the total liabilities of Swiss Banks towards Indians were 1.945 billion Swiss Francs (about ₹ 9,295 crore). The Swiss Ministry of External Affairs confirmed these figures when a reference was made by the Indian Ministry of External Affairs to them". [10] The White Paper further noted, "The illicit money transferred outside India may come back to India through various methods such as hawala, mispricing, foreign direct investment (FDI) through beneficial tax jurisdictions, raising of capital by Indian companies through global depository receipts (GDRs), and investment in Indian stock markets through participatory notes. It is possible that a large amount of money transferred outside India might actually have returned through these means". [11]

Endnotes

1. Under entry 63 of List II (State List) in the Seventh Schedule of the Constitution of India, stamp duty is levied by the State Governments on the registration of property or other conveyances. Till recently, the stamp duty rates were quite high in most states and the procedures for evaluating the conveyances were also

complicated. In this context, the Tenth Five Year Plan (2002-07) remarked, "Stamp duty needs to be paid on all documents which are registered and the rate varies from state to state. With stamp duty rates of 13 percent in Delhi, 14.5 percent in Uttar Pradesh and 12.5 percent in Haryana, India has perhaps one of the highest levels of stamp duty. Some states even have double stamp incidence, first on land and then on its development. In contrast the maximum rate levied in most developed markets whether in Singapore or Europe is in the range of 1-2 percent. Even the National Housing and Habitat Policy, 1998, recommended a stamp duty rate of 2-3 percent. Most of the methods to avoid registration are basically to avoid payment of high stamp duty.

Another fall out of high stamp duty rates is the understatement of the proceeds of a sale. This is also linked to payment of income tax and capital gains tax. When registration has not been effected, a transfer is not deemed to have taken place and hence capital gains tax can be totally avoided. Thus, the present provisions in various laws and their poor implementation have led to a situation where there is considerable financial loss to the exchequer on account of understatement of sale proceeds, non-registration and consequent non-payment of stamp duty and avoidance of capital gains tax". [Government of India, Planning Commission, *Tenth Five Year Plan* (2002-07), Volume II, pp. 833-834.]

Of late, states have undertaken reforms by reducing the duty rates and streamlining procedures for evaluation of property. After the reduction of rates, the general experience has been revenue-augmentation due to improved compliance of law.

2. Derivative in mathematics means a variable derived from another variable. The term *derivative* indicates that it has no independent value, i.e. its value is entirely *derived* from the value of the underlying asset. The underlying asset can be security, commodity, bullion, currency, live stock or anything else. In other words, derivative means a forward, future, option or any other hybrid contract of pre-determined fixed duration, linked for the purpose of contract fulfilment to the value of a specified real or financial asset of an index of securities. Similarly, in the financial sense, a derivative is a financial product, which has been derived from a market for another product. Without the underlying product, derivatives do not have

any independent existence in the market.

Derivative instruments are defined by the Indian Securities Contracts (Regulation) Act, 1956 to include: (i) a security derived from a debt instrument, share, secured/unsecured loan, risk instrument or contract for differences, or any other form of security, and (ii) a contract that derives its value from the prices/index of prices of underlying securities.

3. A participatory note (PN) is a derivative instrument issued in foreign jurisdictions, by a foreign institutional investor (FII)/or one of its associates, against underlying Indian securities.

4. Government of India, Ministry of Finance, *White Paper on Black Money*, 2012, para 2.8.5.

5. National Commission for Enterprises in the Unorganized Sector [NCEUS] (Chairman: Arjun Sengupta), was set up by the Government of India on September 20, 2004, to "review the status of unorganized/informal sector in India including the nature of enterprises, their size, spread and scope, and magnitude of employment". This step was taken to ensure the welfare and well-being of all workers, particularly those in the unorganized sector, who constitute more than 93 percent of workforce. NCEUS prepared and submitted to the Government a number of reports before submitting its final report in 2009.

6. Transfer pricing refers to the price attached to transactions between the divisions (e.g. branches or subsidiaries) of a company. Transfer pricing is usually considered in a global context, particularly in relation to cross-frontier transactions within a multinational company.

7. Globalisation implies widening and deepening integration with the *globe*, i.e. with people and processes abroad. The trend towards the evolution of a global society is generally thought of in economic terms and in terms of the consequences of the revolution in communication technologies. There is undoubtedly much greater economic integration among the nations of the world today. Globalisation is widely seen as the most important factor that could influence economies of nations the world over in the new millennium. The rapid advancement in information technology and communications has made it not just possible but absolutely essential for economies of the world to adapt or fall by the wayside.

8. Input-output analysis, attributed to American economist Wassily

Loentief, examines the interdependence of the production plans and activities of the various industries which constitute an economy. This interdependence arises because each industry employs the outputs of other industries, and its own output in turn is used by other industries. For example, steel is used to make railway wagons and railway wagons are in turn used to transport steel.

An input-output transaction matrix is a framework of data which provides a detailed information on how the final demand for output is related to the requirements placed on individual industries. It thus, highlights the interdependence of various economic sectors (industries) in the production of final output for the economy as a whole.

9. Money in an economy consists partly of currency and partly of bank deposits. The currency and bank deposits that actually circulate are used over and over again in the course of a specified period (say one year). Every time they are used they enter into a price. Therefore, the total amount of purchasing power which enters into the price level depends on the flow (rather than the stock) of money. The flow can be considered in terms of the stock if the latter is multiplied by its velocity of circulation which is defined as the average number of times a unit of money changes hands during the course of one year. If M is the stock of money and V its velocity of circulation, then the flow of money will be MV.

10. Government of India, Ministry of Finance, *White Paper on Black Money,* May 2012, para 2.6.4.

11. *Ibid.,* para 2.4.9.

3

Institutional and Legislative Measures to Curb Black Money

The responsibility of dealing with the challenge of unaccounted wealth and its consequences is jointly and collectively shared by a number of institutions belonging to the Central and State Governments. These various organisátions closely monitor violation of laws regulating economic activities and their links with other criminal activities and in doing so provide a comprehensive network of checks and balances against generation of black money too. However, the federal structure of governance and their vertical reporting systems within their respective ministries and departments may have resulted in less than optimum coordination of data, information, and actions and a strengthening of this aspect may be an important way forward in the fight against generation and accumulation of black money.

3.1 Agencies for Enforcement of Tax Laws

3.1.1 Central Board of Direct Taxes (CBDT):
The CBDT, New Delhi, is part of the Department of Revenue in the Ministry of Finance. While the CBDT provides essential inputs for policy and planning of direct taxes in India, it is also responsible for administration of direct tax laws through its Income Tax Department. The CBDT is a statutory authority functioning under the Central Board of Revenue Act, 1963. The officials of the Board in their ex-officio capacity also function as a Division of the Ministry dealing with matters relating to the levy and collection of direct taxes.

The Income Tax Department is primarily responsible for combating the menace of black money. For this purpose, it uses the tools of scrutiny assessment as well as information-based investigations for detecting tax evasion and penalising the same as per provisions of the Income Tax Act, 1961 with the objective of creating deterrence against tax evasion. In doing so, it plays one of the most important roles in preventing generation, accumulation, and consumption of unaccounted black money.

The Investigation Wing of the Income Tax Department deals with investigations to detect tax evasion and carries out operations like surveys and searches to collect evidence of such evasion. Such operations are usually carried out after detailed preliminary investigations and in cases involving substantial evasion of taxes.

A. Directorate of Criminal Investigation (DCI): Till recently, the tax administration in India did not have a separate set-up for targeted investigation into criminal cases. On May 30, 2011, a notification was issued by the Government of India for creation of a Directorate of Income Tax (Criminal Investigation) or DCI in the Central Board of Direct Taxes, Department of Revenue, Ministry of Finance. The DCI is mandated to perform functions in respect of criminal matters having any financial implication punishable as an offence under any direct taxes law.

The DCI, in discharge of its responsibilities under the direct tax laws, is required to perform the following functions:

1. Seek and collect information about persons and transactions suspected to be involved in criminal activities having cross-border, inter-state, or international ramifications that pose a threat to national security and are punishable under the direct tax laws.
2. Investigate the sources and uses of funds involved in such criminal activities.
3. Cause issuance of show cause notices for offences committed under any direct tax law.
4. File prosecution complaints in the competent court under any direct tax law relating to a criminal activity.
5. Hire the services of special prosecutors and other experts for pursuing a prosecution complaint filed in any court of

competent jurisdiction.

6. Execute appropriate witness protection programmes for effective prosecution of criminal offences under the direct tax laws, i.e. to protect and rehabilitate witnesses who support the state in prosecution of such offences so as to insulate them from any harm to their person.

7. Coordinate with and extend necessary expert, technical, and logistical support to any other intelligence or law enforcement agency in India investigating crimes having cross-border, inter-state or international ramifications that pose a threat to national security.

8. Enter into agreements for sharing of information and other cooperation with any central or state agency in India.

9. Enter into agreements for sharing of information and other cooperation with such agencies of foreign states as may be permissible under any international agreement or treaty.

10. Any other matter relating to the above.

The DCI is headed by a Director General of Income Tax (Criminal Investigation) and functions under administrative control of the CBDT. The head office of the DCI is located at New Delhi and it has eight regional offices all over India.

B. Exchange of Information (EoI) Cell: The Government of India has set up an EoI Cell in CBDT. The EoI works on the basis of mutual cooperation. The competent authorities of different countries provide different forms of administrative assistance to each other based on the provisions of Double Tax Avoidance Agreements (DTAAs) or the Multilateral Convention for Mutual Administrative Assistance. Administrative assistance under these instruments of EOI, depending on the terms of the agreement, may take the form of: (a) specific exchange of information, (b) spontaneous exchange of information, (c) automatic exchange of information, (d) tax examination abroad, (e) simultaneous exchange of information, (f) service of documents, and (g) assistance in collection of tax.

C. Income Tax Overseas Units (ITOUs): With increased scope for international cooperation in areas of exchange of information, transfer pricing, and taxation of cross-border transactions, Government of India decided to create a network of ITOUs. In addition to the existing two ITOUs at Singapore and Mauritius, eight more have been opened. The objectives of these ITOUs are as under:

1. Monitor DTAA-related issues.
2. Assist the authorities in handling issues arising out of international taxation and transfer pricing.
3. Assist the authorities in frequent revision of existing DTAAs.
4. Assist the authorities in negotiation of TIEAs.
5. Expedite the exchange of information by the competent authorities (as per DTAAs and TIEAs) of these countries as required by the competent authority in India.
6. Assist the authorities in collection of taxes.
7. Assist the authorities in work relating to Mutual Agreement Procedure under DTAAs.
8. Maintain liaison with various departments of the respective countries especially income tax department, registrar of companies, department of banking services, and administrators of financial services.
9. Maintain liaison with investors investing in India from these countries.
10. Impart information about domestic laws of India to foreign investors.
11. Maintain liaison with Indian investors in these countries to assess any tax-related problems arising for these investors.
12. Assist the Mission in any other commercial/economic work assigned to the officer by the Head of the Mission.
13. Any other work assigned to the officer by the CBDT, Department of Revenue.

Opening of the new ITOUs and presence of tax officers in the ITOUs also acts as effective deterrence against tax evasion.

3.1.2 Central Board of Excise and Customs (CBEC): The CBEC is a part of the Department of Revenue under the Ministry of Finance, Government of India. It deals with the tasks of formulation of policy concerning levy and collection of customs and central excise duties, prevention of smuggling, and administration of matters relating to customs, central excise and narcotics to the extent under the CBEC's purview. The Board is the administrative authority for its subordinate organizations, including Custom Houses, Central Excise Commissionerates, and the Central Revenues Control Laboratory.

The Directorate General of Central Excise Intelligence (DGCEI) is the apex intelligence organization functioning under the CBEC. It is entrusted with the responsibility of detecting cases of evasion of central excise and service tax. The Directorate develops intelligence, especially in new areas of tax evasion through its intelligence network across the country and disseminates information in this respect by issuing modus operandi circulars and alert circulars to apprise field formations of the latest trends in duty evasion. Wherever found necessary, DGCEI on its own, or in coordination with field formations, organises operations to unearth evasion of central excise duty and service tax.

3.2 Regulatory Authorities for Supervision and Policing

3.2.1 Central Bureau of Investigation (CBI): CBI, functioning under the Department of Personnel, Ministry of Personnel, Pension and Public Grievances, Government of India, is the premier investigating police agency in India. It handles a broad category of criminal cases including cases of corruption and fraud committed by public servants, economic crimes, and other specific crimes involving terrorism, bomb blasts, sensational homicides, kidnappings and the underworld. The CBI plays an important role in international cooperation relating to mutual legal assistance and extradition matters. The Ministry of Home Affairs is the central authority for mutual legal assistance in criminal matters and the Ministry of External Affairs, the nodal agency for extradition matters.

3.2.2 Financial Intelligence Unit (FIU): The FIU-IND was established by the Government of India on November 18, 2004 for coordinating and strengthening efforts for national and international intelligence by investigation and enforcement agencies in combating money laundering and terrorist financing. FIU-IND is the national agency responsible for receiving, processing, analysing, and disseminating information relating to suspect financial transactions. It is an independent body reporting to the Economic Intelligence Council headed by the Finance Minister. For administrative purposes, the FIU-IND is under the control of the Department of Revenue, Ministry of Finance.

3.2.3 Narcotics Control Bureau (NCB): It functions under the Ministry of Home Affairs, Government of India. It was established on March 17, 1986 and its functions include co-ordination of actions by various offices, state governments, and other authorities under the Narcotics Drugs and Psychotropic Substances (NDPS) Act, 1985, Customs Act, Drugs and Cosmetics Act, and any other law for the time being in force in connection with the enforcement provisions of the NDPS Act. It is assigned the task of counter measures against illicit drugs traffic under the various international conventions and protocols, and also assists concerned authorities in foreign countries and concerned international organisations dealing with prevention and suppression of this traffic.

3.3 Co-ordinating Agencies
3.3.1 Central Economic Intelligence Bureau (CEIB): The CEIB functioning under the Ministry of Finance is responsible for coordination, intelligence sharing, and investigations at national as well as regional levels amongst various law enforcement agencies. The existing coordination mechanism in the CEIB consists of Regional Economic Intelligence Councils (REICs) at regional level and the Group on Economic Intelligence and meetings of the heads of investigating agencies under the Department of Revenue at the centre. While the Group on Economic Intelligence is focused on matters relating to intelligence sharing, the REICs and heads of agencies meetings cover both intelligence and investigations.

3.3.2 National Investigation Agency (NIA): It is a specialised and dedicated investigating agency set up under the National Investigation Agency Act to investigate and prosecute scheduled offences, in particular offences under the Unlawful Activities (Prevention) Act, including financing of terrorism. The NIA has concurrent jurisdiction with the individual states, thereby empowering the Central Government to probe terror attacks in any part of the country. Officers of the NIA have all powers, privileges, and liabilities which police officers have in connection with investigation of an offence.

The Central Government has the power to suo moto assign a case to the NIA for investigation. The NIA Act also provides for setting up of special courts and trials to be held on a day-to-day basis. The NIA Act can investigate offences under the specific Acts mentioned in the Schedule to NIA Act, including the Atomic Energy Act, 1962; Unlawful Activities (Prevention) Act, 1967; Anti-Hijacking Act, 1982; Suppression of Unlawful Acts against Safety of Civil Aviation Act, 1982; SAARC Convention (Suppression of Terrorism) Act, 1993; Suppression of Unlawful Acts against Safety of Maritime Navigation and Fixed Platforms on Continental Shelf Act, 2002; Weapons of Mass Destruction and Their Delivery Systems (Prohibition of Unlawful Activities) Act, 2005; and offences under Chapter VI and Sections 489-A to 489-E of the Indian Penal Code.

3.4 Other Agencies

3.4.1 Central Bureau of Narcotics (CBN): It supervises the cultivation of opium poppy in India and issues necessary licences for manufacture, export and import of narcotics drugs and psychotropic substances. It monitors India's implementation of the United Nations Drug Control Conventions and also interacts with the International Narcotics Control Board (INCB) in Vienna and the competent authorities of other countries to verify the genuineness of a transaction prior to authorising shipments.

3.4.2 Serious Frauds Investigation Office (SFIO): It functions under the Ministry of Corporate Affairs and takes up for investigation complex cases having inter-departmental and multidisciplinary ramifications and substantial involvement of public interest, either in terms of monetary misappropriation or in terms of persons affected. It also takes up cases where investigation has the potential of contributing towards a clear improvement in systems, laws, or procedures.

3.4.3 Registrar of Companies (RoCs): It is the Registry for companies and limited liability firms and is established under the Ministry of Corporate Affairs. The Ministry of Corporate Affairs has a three-tier organisational set-up consisting of a Secretariat in New Delhi, Regional Directorates in Mumbai, Kolkata, Chennai and Noida, and field offices in all states and union territories.

3.4.4 Registrar of Societies (RoSs): The Registrars of non-profit societies are within State Government's purview and most of the states have a RoS office. The Society Registration Act is a Central Act but many states have adopted it with some state amendments and are registering non-profit societies under their respective Acts. Some state assemblies have enacted completely separate legislation on the subject. The RoS offices are reservoirs of data on societies and also function as their regulator.

3.4.5 Economic Intelligence Council (EIC): It came into existence in 2003 and is chaired by the Finance Minister and comprises senior functionaries of various ministries and intelligence agencies, including the Governor of the Reserve Bank of India (RBI) and the Chairman of Securities and Exchange Board of India (SEBI). The EIC meets at least once a year to discuss and take decisions regarding trends in economic offences and strategies on intelligence sharing, coordination etc. The implementation of decisions taken by the EIC is monitored by the Working Group on Intelligence Apparatus, set up for this purpose within the EIC.

3.4.6 National Crime Records Bureau (NCRB): It was set up with the objective of empowering the Indian police services with information technology and criminal intelligence with a view to enabling them to effectively and efficiently enforce the law. It therefore, creates and maintains a secured national database on crimes, criminals, property, and organised criminal gangs for use by law enforcement agencies.

The NCRB also processes and disseminates fingerprint records of criminals, including foreign criminals, to establish their identity.

3.4.7 State Police Agencies: Under the Constitution of India, police and public order are state (provincial) subjects. Every State/Union Territory has its own police force, which performs not only normal policing duties but also has specialised units to combat economic offences. The Economic Offences Wing (EOW) of the police functioning under the administrative control of states (provinces) is entrusted with the responsibility of investigation of serious economic offences and offences having inter-state ramifications.

3.5 Recent Legislative Measures to Prevent Generation of Black Money

A number of proactive steps have recently been taken in order to create an appropriate legislative framework for preventing the generation of black money and for its detection.

3.5.1 Prevention of Money Laundering Act (PMLA), 2002: *Money laundering* is the process of transforming the proceeds of crime and corruption into ostensibly legitimate assets. In a number of legal and regulatory systems, however, the term money laundering has become conflated with other forms of financial and business crime, and is sometimes used more generally to include misuse of the financial system, including terrorism financing and evasion of international sanctions. Most anti-money laundering laws openly conflate money laundering with terrorism financing when regulating the financial system.

Some countries define money laundering as obfuscating sources of money, either intentionally or by merely using financial systems or services that do not identify or track sources or destinations. Other countries define money laundering to include money from activity that *would have been* a crime in that country, even if it was legal where the actual conduct occurred. This broad brush of applying money laundering to incidental, extraterritorial or simply privacy-seeking behaviours has led some to label it *financial thought crime*.

PMLA was enacted to prevent money laundering and provide for confiscation of property derived from, or involved in, money laundering and for matters connected therewith or incidental thereto. The Act also addresses international obligations under the Political Declaration and Global Programme of Action adopted by the General Assembly of the United Nations to prevent money laundering.

To strengthen the provisions of the PMLA, amendments were carried out in 2009. These amendments have introduced new definitions to clarify and strengthen the Act and strengthened provisions related to attachment of property involved in money laundering and its seizure and confiscation. More offences have been added in Parts A and B of the Schedule to the Act, including those pertaining to insider trading and market manipulation as well as smuggling of antiques, terrorism funding, human trafficking other than prostitution, and a wider range of environmental crimes. A new category of offences with cross-border implications has been introduced as Part C.

The problem of black money is no longer restricted to the geo-political boundaries of any country. It has become a global menace that cannot be contained by any nation alone. In view of this, India has become a member of the Financial Action Task Force (FATF) [1] and Asia/Pacific Group on Money Laundering (APG) [2] which are committed to the effective implementation and enforcement of internationally accepted standards against money laundering and the financing of terrorism. Consequent to the submission of an action plan to the FATF for bringing India's anti-money laundering legislation on par with international standards and to address some of the deficiencies of the Act that have been experienced by the implementing agencies, PMLA 2002 is further proposed to be amended through the Prevention of Money Laundering (Amendment) Bill 2011, which is under consideration of Parliament. The Bill seeks to introduce the concept of *corresponding law* to link the provisions of Indian law with the laws of foreign countries and provide for transfer of the proceeds of the foreign predicate offence in any manner in India. It also proposes to enlarge the definition of the offence of money laundering to include therein activities like concealment, acquisition, possession, and use of proceeds of crime as criminal activities and remove the existing limit of ₹ 5 lakh for imposition of fine under the Act.

It also strengthens provisions for attachment and confiscation of the proceeds of crime and widens the investigative powers of the concerned officials and clubs offences listed under Schedules A and B into a single Schedule.

A. Anti-money Laundering Guidelines: In recent years, prevention of money laundering has assumed importance in international financial relationships. In this context, in November 2004, the RBI revised the guidelines on know your customer (KYC) principles in line with the recommendations made by the Financial Action Task Force (FATF) on anti-money laundering (AML) standards and combating financing of terrorism (CFT). Banks were advised to frame their KYC policies with the approval of their Boards and ensure they are compliant with its provisions by December 31, 2005. The salient features of the policy relate to the procedure prescribed with regard to: (a) customer acceptance, (b) customer identification, (c) risk management, and (d) monitoring as required under Prevention of Money Laundering Act (PMLA), 2002.

The revised guidelines make the verification of the identity of the customer and address through independent source documents mandatory. Banks are also required to classify the accounts according to the risk perceived by the bank. However, in order to ensure that the inability of persons belonging to low income groups to produce documents to establish their identity and address does not lead to their financial exclusion and denial of banking services, simplified procedure has been provided for opening of accounts for those persons who do not intend to keep balances above ₹ 50,000 and whose total credit in one year is not expected to exceed ₹ 1,00,000. In addition, the RBI issued instructions emphasising the obligation on banks to follow the provisions of the Foreign Contribution (Regulation) Act, 1976 in respect of acceptance of foreign donations on behalf of associations/organisations maintaining accounts with them.

In November 2004, the RBI revised the guidelines on know your customer (KYC) principles in line with the recommendations made by the Financial Action Task Force (FATF) on standards for anti-money laundering (AML) and combating financing of terrorism (CFT).

3.5.2 Benami Transactions (Prohibition) Amendment Act, 2016: It came into force from November 1, 2016. The new law seeks to give more teeth to the authorities to curb benami transactions and hence black money. The Act is an amendment of the existing Benami Transactions (Prohibition) Act, 1988. After coming into force, it was renamed as Prohibition of Benami Property Transactions Act, 1988 (PBPT Act). The Act defines *benami* transactions and also provides imprisonment up to 7 years and fine for violation of the Act. The earlier law provided for up to 3 years of imprisonment or fine or both.

The PBPT Act prohibits recovery of the property held benami from benamidar by the real owner. Properties held benami are liable for confiscation by the government without payment of compensation. The new law also provides for an appellate mechanism in the form of an adjudicating authority and appellate tribunal.

The amendments aim to strengthen the Act in terms of legal and administrative procedure. The *benami* (without a name) property refers to property purchased by a person in the name of some other person. The person on whose name the property is purchased is called the *benamdar* and the property so purchased is called the *benami* property. The person who finances the deal is the real owner.

The PBPT Act prohibits recovery of the property held benami from benamdar by the real owner. As per the Act, properties held benami are liable for confiscation by the government, without payment of compensation. An appellate mechanism has been provided under the act, in the form of an adjudicating authority and appellate tribunal.

The four authorities who will conduct inquiries or investigations are the Initiating Officer, Approving Authority, Administrator and Adjudicating Authority.

In the case of charitable or religious organisation properties, the government has the power to grant exemption.

A. Highlights of the Act: (a) Up to 7 years imprisonment and fine for indulging in benami transactions, (b) furnishing false information is punishable by imprisonment up to 5 years and fine, (c) properties held benami are liable for confiscation by government without compensation, (d) initiating officer may pass an order to continue holding the property and may then refer case to adjudicating authority, (e) adjudicating authority will then examine evidence and pass an order, (f) appellate tribunal will hear appeals against orders of adjudicating authority, and (g) High Court to hear appeals against orders of appellate tribunal.

3.5.3 Public Procurement Bill: The Public Procurement Bill 2012 was approved by the Union Cabinet on April 12, 2012 for introduction in the Parliament. The Bill seeks to regulate procurement by ministries/departments of the Central Government and its attached/subordinate offices, Central public sector enterprises (CPSEs), autonomous and statutory bodies controlled by the Central Government and other procuring entities with the objectives of ensuring transparency, accountability and probity in the procurement process, fair and equitable treatment of bidders, promoting competition, enhancing efficiency and economy, safeguarding integrity in the procurement process, and enhancing public confidence in public procurement.

The Bill is based on broad principles and envisages a set of detailed rules, guidelines, and model documents. It builds on national and international experience and best practices as appropriate for the needs of the Government of India. It will create a statutory framework for public procurement which will provide greater accountability, transparency, and enforceability of the regulatory framework. The Bill codifies the essential principles governing procurement required for achieving economy, efficiency, and quality as well as combating corruption. It legally obligates procuring entities and their officials to comply with these principles. It also ensures that competition will be maximised in procurement, while providing for adequate flexibility for different types of procurement needs. It puts in place a strong framework of transparency and accountability through a public procurement portal and a grievance redressal system in which an independent mechanism, chaired by a retired High Court Judge, will review grievances.

Minister of Finance Arun Jaitley's 2015-16 budget speech signalled the government's commitment to formally legalise India's public procurement system as a part of its continuing reforms in public financial management. Following this, the Government is seeking suggestions to refine the Public Procurement Bill of 2012, introduced by the previous government.

3.5.4 Prevention of Bribery of Foreign Public Officials and Officials of the Public International Organisations Bill 2011: India had signed the United Nations Convention against Corruption on December 9, 2005. This Bill became necessary for the ratification of the Convention. It provides a mechanism to deal with bribery among foreign public officials (FPO) and officials of public international organizations (OPIO).

This Bill was introduced in the Lok Sabha on March 25, 2011. The Bill seeks to prevent corruption relating to bribery of foreign public officials and officials of public international organisations and to address matters connected therewith or incidental thereto. The proposed legislation prohibits acceptance of gratification by foreign public officials or officials of public international organisations as well as the act of giving such gratification or its abetment. The bill also empowers the Central Government to enter into agreements with foreign countries for enforcing the provisions, makes offences under the proposed act extraditable, and provides for attachment, seizure and confiscation of property in India or the respective country and mutual assistance in this regard.

The Bill lapsed with the dissolution of the 15th Lok Sabha in May 2014. A bill that makes accepting or giving bribe by foreign public officials a criminal offence entailing imprisonment of up to 7 years among other strict penal provisions will be moved afresh in the Parliament by the government.

3.5.5 Lokpal and Lokayuktas Act, 2013: Commonly known as Lokpal Act, it is an anti-corruption Act of Indian Parliament which seeks to provide for the establishment of the institution of Lokpal to inquire into allegations of corruption against certain public functionaries and for matters connecting them.

The Act creates a Lokpal at the centre which shall consist of a chairperson and up to eight members. Half of these members should have higher judicial experience and the other half should have experience in public administration, finance, insurance and banking laws, anti-corruption and vigilance. It also provides that half the members of Lokpal shall be from amongst scheduled castes, scheduled tribes, other backward castes, minority communities and women. The chairman and members of Lokpal shall be appointed by a selection committee consisting of the Prime Minister, the Speaker of Lok Sabha, the Leader of Opposition in Lok Sabha, the Chief Justice of India or a sitting supreme court judge as nominated by the CJI and an eminent jurist to be nominated by the President based on the recommendations of the other members of the selection committee.

The Act specifies that the office of Lokpal shall investigate and prosecute cases of corruption. The jurisdiction of Lokpal extends to the Prime Minister, Ministers, current and former Members of Parliament and Members of Legislative Assemblies, government employees and employees of companies funded or controlled by the central or state government. Lokpal shall also have jurisdiction over institutions receiving foreign donations in excess of ten lakh rupees per year or such higher limit as specified. The Act excludes, any allegation of corruption against a Member of Parliament in respect of anything said or a vote given in Parliament, from the jurisdiction of Lokpal.

The legislation provides an imprisonment of up to seven years for public servants on grounds of corruption. Criminal misconduct and habitually abetting corruption has a higher penalty and would result in imprisonment up to ten years. Making false and frivolous complaints to Lokpal would result in a fine of up to one lakh rupees and imprisonment of up to one year. In addition a person who is convicted for having made a false complaint shall be liable to compensate the public servant against whom the false complaint was made. However complaints made in good faith, that is with due care, caution and a sense of responsibility will be excluded from penalty.

3.5.6 Citizens' Grievance Redressal Bill: The Right of Citizens for Time Bound Delivery of Goods and Services and Redressal of their Grievances Bill, 2011, outlines the responsibilities of government departments towards citizens and how someone who is denied the service due to him can seek redressal. It mandates that every public authority or government department has to publish a citizen's charter listing all services rendered by that department along with a grievance redressal mechanism for non-compliance with the citizen's charter. It also sets up a Central Public Grievances Redressal Commission, with an equivalent in every state, and provides for a designated authority from a department other than the one against which the complaint has been filed to address the complaint.

The Bill lapsed due to dissolution of the 15th Lok Sabha in May 2014.

3.5.7 Judicial Standards and Accountability Bill, 2010:

It was passed by the Lok Sabha and is under consideration of the Rajya Sabha. The Bill provides a mechanism for enquiring into complaints against judges of the Supreme Court and High Courts, lays down judicial standards, and requires judges of the Supreme Court and High Courts to declare their assets and liabilities. The Bill seeks to replace the Judges (Inquiry) Act 1968 while retaining its basic features. The enactment of the Bill will address the growing concerns regarding the need to ensure greater accountability of the higher judiciary by bringing in more transparency and will further strengthen the credibility and independence of the judiciary. The Bill seeks to lay down enforceable standards of conduct for judges. The main features of the Bill are as under:

1. It requires judges to declare their assets, lays down judicial standards, and establishes processes for removal of judges of the Supreme Court and High Courts.

2. It requires judges to declare their assets and liabilities and also those of their spouses and children.

3. The Bill establishes the National Judicial Oversight Committee, the Complaints Scrutiny Panel, and an investigation committee. Any person can make a complaint against a judge to the Oversight Committee on grounds of *misbehaviour*.

4. A motion for removal of a judge on grounds of misbehaviour can also be moved in Parliament. Such a motion will be referred for further inquiry to the Oversight Committee.

5. Complaints and inquiries against judges will be confidential and frivolous complaints will be penalised.

6. The Oversight Committee may issue advisories or warnings to judges and also recommend their removal to the President.

The Judicial Standards and Accountability Bill was brought by the previous UPA government but had lapsed following the dissolution of the 15th Lok Sabha in May 2014.

The NDA government is planning to revive the bill, which sought to put in place a system to probe complaints against judges of the Supreme Court and the High Courts, after adding a new clause to assess the performance of members of the higher judiciary.

3.5.8 Whistle Blowers Protection Act, 2011: This Act provides a mechanism to investigate alleged corruption and misuse of power by public servants and also protect anyone who exposes alleged wrongdoing in government bodies, projects and offices. The wrongdoing might take the form of fraud, corruption or mismanagement. The Act will also ensure punishment for false or frivolous complaints.

The Act was approved by the Cabinet of India as part of a drive to eliminate corruption in the country's bureaucracy and passed by the Lok Sabha on December 27, 2011. The Bill was passed by Rajya Sabha on February 21, 2014 and received the President's assent on May 9, 2014.

A. Salient Features: These are as under:

1. The Act seeks to protect whistle blowers, i.e. persons making a public interest disclosure related to an act of corruption, misuse of power, or criminal offence by a public servant.
2. Any public servant or any other person including a non-governmental organization may make such a disclosure to the Central or State Vigilance Commission.
3. Every complaint has to include the identity of the complainant.
4. The Vigilance Commission shall not disclose the identity of the complainant except to the head of the department if he deems it necessary. The Act penalizes any person who has disclosed the identity of the complainant.

The Act prescribes penalties for knowingly making false complaints.

3.5.9 Electronic Delivery of Services Bill, 2011: It seeks to provide for electronic delivery of public services by the Government to all persons to ensure transparency, efficiency, accountability, accessibility and reliability in delivery of such services. It was tabled before the Parliament in December 2011.

The Bill aims to provide access to all Central and State

Government services such as passport, ration card and driving licences electronically, especially through the Internet, within 8 years.

The Bill lapsed due to dissolution of the 15th Lok Sabha in May 2014.

To sum up, prevention and control of black money generation is a pre-requisite to establish an equitable, transparent and a more efficient economy. The factors leading to generation of black money in India —along with the various measures attempted to counter it—make it clear that there is no single remedy to curb, control, and finally prevent the generation of black money. In fact, a comprehensive mix of well-defined strategies is needed by the Central and State Governments and put into practice by all their agencies in a co-ordinated manner.

The fight against the menace of black money has to be at ethical, socio-economic and administrative levels. At the ethical level, we have to reinforce value/moral education in the school curriculum and build good character citizens, particularly highlighting the ills of tax evasion and black money. At the socio-economic level, the thrust of public policy should be to discourage conspicuous and wasteful consumption/expenditure, encourage savings, frugality and simplicity, and reduce the gap between the rich and the poor.

Endnotes
1. See section 2.2.6 of chapter 2 of this book.
2. See section 2.2.7 of chapter 2 of this book.

4

Economics of Digitization and Digital India (DI): Vision 2019

4.1 Economics of Digitization

The economics of digitization is the field of economics that studies how digitization affects markets and how digital data can be used to study economics. Digitization is the process by which technology lowers the costs of storing, sharing, and analyzing data. This process has changed how consumers behave, how industrial activity is organized, and how governments operate. The economics of digitization exists as a distinct field of economics for two reasons. First, new economic models are needed because many traditional assumptions about information no longer hold in a digitized world. Second, the new types of data generated by digitization require new methods to analyze.

Research in the economics of digitization touches on several fields of economics including industrial organization, labour economics, and intellectual property. Consequently, many of the contributions to the economics of digitization have also found an intellectual home in these fields. An underlying theme in much of the work in the field is that existing government regulation of copyright, security, and anti-trust is inappropriate in the modern world. For example, information goods, such as news articles and movies, now have zero marginal cost of production and sharing. This has made the piracy of information goods common and has increased competition between providers of information goods. Research in the economics of digitization studies how policy should adapt in response to these changes.

A key issue in the economics of digitization is how much people value internet-based services. The motivation for this question is two-fold. First, economists are interested in understanding digitization related policies such as network infrastructure investment and subsidies for internet access. Second, economists want to measure the gains to consumers from the internet. This is an especially important topic because many economists believe that traditional measures of economic growth, such as GDP, understate the true benefits of improving technology.

Digitization has coincided with the increased prominence of platforms and marketplaces that connect diverse agents in social and economic activity. Platforms are most readily identified with their technical standards, i.e. engineering specifications for hardware and standards for software. The pricing and product strategies that platforms use differ from those of traditional firms because of the presence of network effects. Network effects are within platforms because participation by one group affects the utility of another group. Furthermore, network effects make the analysis of competition between platforms more complex than the analysis of competition between traditional firms. Much work in the economics of digitization studies the question of how these firms should operate and how they compete with each other. A particularly important issue is whether successful online platforms should be subject to anti-trust actions.

Digitization has partially or fully replaced many tasks that were previously done by human labourers. At the same time, computers have made some workers much more productive. Economists are interested in understanding how these two forces interact in determining labour market outcomes. For example, a large literature studies the magnitude and causes of skill-biased technical change, the process by which technology improves wages for educated workers.

Another consequence of digitization is that it has drastically reduced the costs of communication between workers across different organizations and locations. This has led to a change in the geographic and contractual organization of production.

Privacy and data security is an area where digitization has

substantially changed the costs and benefits to various economic actors. Traditional policies regarding privacy circumscribed the ability of government agencies to access individual data. However, the large-scale ability of firms to collect, parse, and analyze detailed micro-level data about consumers has shifted the policy focus. Now, the concern is whether access consumer data of firms should be regulated and restricted or not.

There are many other policies related to digitization that are of interest to economists. For example, digitization may affect government effectiveness and accountability. Digitization also makes it easier for firms in one jurisdiction to supply consumers in another. This creates challenges for tax enforcement. Many safety and quality enforcement regulations may no longer be necessary with the advent of online reputation systems. Lastly, digitization is of great importance to health care policy. For example, electronic medical records have the potential to make healthcare more effective but pose challenges to privacy policy.

4.2 Digital Economy and Knowledge Economy

4.2.1 Digital Economy: It refers to an economy that is based on digital technologies. The digital economy is also sometimes called the *internet economy*, *new economy*, or *web economy*. Increasingly, the *digital economy* is intertwined with the traditional economy making a clear delineation harder.

In this new economy, digital networking and communication infrastructures provide a global platform over which people and organizations devise strategies, interact, communicate, collaborate and search for information.

It is widely accepted that the growth of the digital economy has widespread impact on the whole economy. Various attempts at categorising the size of the impact on traditional sectors have been made.

Given its expected broad impact, traditional firms are actively assessing how to respond to the changes brought about by the digital economy. For corporations, timing of their response is of the essence. Banks are trying to innovate and use digital tools to improve their traditional business.

4.2.2 Knowledge Economy: Knowledge economy is the use of knowledge to generate tangible and intangible values. Technology and in particular knowledge technology help to transform a part of human knowledge to machines. This knowledge can be used by decision support systems in various fields and generate economic values. Knowledge economy is also possible without technology.

Other than the agricultural-intensive economies and labour-intensive economies, the global economy is in transition to a *knowledge economy*, as an extension of an *information society* in the information age led by innovation. The transition requires that the rules and practices that determined success in the industrial economy need rewriting in an interconnected, globalized economy where knowledge resources such as trade secrets and expertise are as critical as other economic resources.

A key concept of the knowledge economy is that knowledge and education (often referred to as *human capital*) can be treated as one of the following two:

• A business product, as educational and innovative intellectual products and services can be exported for a high value return.

• A productive asset.

It can be defined as products and services based on knowledge-intensive activities that contribute to an accelerated pace of technical and scientific advance, as well as rapid obsolescence. The key component of a knowledge economy is a greater reliance on intellectual capabilities than on physical inputs or natural resources.

The key problem in the formalization and modelling of knowledge economy is a vague definition of *knowledge*, which is a rather relative concept. For example, it is not proper to consider *information society* as interchangeable with *knowledge society*. *Information* is usually not equivalent to *knowledge*. Their use, as well, depends on individual and group *preferences*.

The knowledge economy is also seen as the latest stage of development in global economic restructuring. Thus far, the developed world has transitioned from an agricultural economy to industrial economy to post-industrial/mass production economy to knowledge economy. This latest stage has been marked by the upheavals in technological innovations and the globally competitive need for innovation with new products and processes that develop from the research community.

In the knowledge economy, the specialized labour force is characterized as computer literate and well-trained in handling data, developing algorithms and simulated models, and innovating on processes and systems. Consequently, computer scientists, engineers, chemists, biologists, mathematicians, and scientific inventors will see continuous demand in years to come. Hence, knowledge is the catalyst and connective tissue in modern economies.

Knowledge provides the technical expertise, problem-solving, performance measurement and evaluation, and data management needed for the trans-boundary, interdisciplinary global scale of today's competition.

Worldwide examples of the knowledge economy taking place among many others include: Silicon Valley (California, US); aerospace and automotive engineering (Munich, Germany); biotechnology (Hyderabad, India); electronics and digital media (Seoul, South Korea); and petrochemical and energy industry in (Brazil).

It has been suggested that the next evolutionary step after knowledge economy is the network economy, where the relatively localized knowledge is now being shared among and across various networks for the benefit of the network members as a whole.

The knowledge economy has manifold forms in which it may appear but there are predictions that the new economy will extend radically, creating a pattern in which even ideas will be recognised and identified as a commodity. This certainly is not the best time to make any hasty judgment on this contention, but considering the very nature of *knowledge* itself, added to the fact that it is the thrust of this new form of economy, there certainly is a clear way forward for this notion, though the particulars remain in the speculative realm, as of now.

4.3 Digital India (DI): Vision 2019

Digital India is an initiative of the Government of India to integrate Government Ministries/Departments with the people of India. It aims at ensuring the availability of government services to citizens electronically by reducing paperwork. The initiative also includes plans to connect rural areas with high-speed internet networks. DI has three core components. These include creation of digital infrastructure, delivering services digitally and digital literacy.

The project, being handled by the Department of Electronics and Information Technology of the Ministry of Communications and Information Technology, is slated for completion by 2019. A two-way platform will be created where both the service providers and the consumers stand to benefit. The scheme will be monitored and controlled by the *Digital India Advisory Group* which will be chaired by the Ministry of Communications and Information Technology. It is an inter-ministerial initiative where all Ministries and Departments will offer their own services to the public such as healthcare, education, judicial services etc. The Public-Private-Partnership (PPP) model will be adopted selectively. In addition, there are plans to restructure the National Informatics Centre (NIC). This project is one among the top priority projects of Prime Minister Narendra Modi.

The Government of India entity Bharat Broadband Network Limited (BBNL) which executes the National Optical Fibre Network project will be the custodian of DI project. BBNL has ordered United Telecoms Limited to connect 2,50,000 villages through GPON to ensure FTTH based broadband. This will provide the first basic set up to implement DI project and is expected to be completed by 2017.

4.3.1 What is Digital India? Digital India is a programme to transform India into a digitally empowered society and knowledge economy. It has the following components:

1. Digital India is a programme to prepare India for a knowledge future.
2. The focus is on being transformative–to realize IT + IT = IT.
3. The focus is on making technology central to enabling change.
4. It is an Umbrella Programme, covering many departments.
- It weaves together a large number of ideas and thoughts into a single, comprehensive vision so that each of them is seen as part of a larger goal.
- Each individual element stands on its own. But is also part of the larger picture.
- It is coordinated by DeitY, implemented by the entire government.
- The weaving together makes the Mission transformative in totality
5. The Programme:
- Pulls together many existing schemes.
- These schemes will be restructured and re-focused.
- They will be implemented in a synchronized manner.
- Many elements are only process improvements with minimal cost.
6. The common branding of programmes as Digital India highlights their transformative impact.

4.3.2 Vision of Digital India: The Vision of Digital India is centered on the following 3 key areas:

1. Digital infrastructure as a utility to every citizen.
2. Governance and services on demand.
3. Digital empowerment of citizens.

A. Vision Area 1: Infrastructure as Utility to Every Citizen
- High speed internet as a core utility.
- Cradle to grave digital identity: unique, lifelong, online, authenticable.
- Mobile phone and bank account enabling participation in

digital and financial space.

- Easy access to a Common Service Centre.
- Shareable private space on a public cloud.
- Safe and secure cyber space.

B. Vision Area 2: Governance and Services on Demand

- Seamlessly integrated across departments or jurisdictions.
- Services available in real time from online and mobile platform.
- All citizen entitlements to be available on the cloud.
- Services digitally transformed for improving *Ease of Doing Business.*
- Making financial transactions electronic and cashless.
- Leveraging GIS for decision support systems and development.

C. Vision Area 3: Digital Empowerment of Citizens

- Universal digital literacy.
- Universally accessible digital resources.
- All documents/certificates to be available on cloud.
- Availability of digital resources and services in Indian languages.
- Collaborative digital platforms for participative governance.
- Portability of all entitlements through cloud.

4.3.3 Nine Pillars of Digital India

1. Broadband highways.
2. Universal access to phones.
3. Public Internet access programme.
4. E-Governance–reforming government through technology.
5. eKranti—electronic delivery of services.
6. Information for all.
7. Electronics manufacturing–target NET ZERO imports.
8. IT for jobs.
9. Early harvest programmes.

A. Pillar 1: Broadband Highways

- **Broadband for all Rural**

A. Coverage: 2,50,000 GP.

B. Timeline: December 2016.
C. CAPEX: ₹ 32,000 crore.
D. Nodal Department: DoT.
- **Broadband for all Urban**
A. Virtual network operators for service delivery.
B. Mandate communication infrastructure in new urban development and buildings.
- **National Information Infrastructure**
A. Coverage: Nationwide.
B. Timeline: March 2017.
C. Cost: ₹ 15,686 crore.
D. Nodal Department: DeitY.

B. Pillar 2. Universal Access to Mobile Connectivity
- **Universal Access to Mobile Connectivity**
A. Coverage: Remaining uncovered villages (~ 42,300 villages).
B. Timeline: 2014-18.
C. Cost: ₹ 16,000 crore.
D. Nodal Department: DoT.

C. Pillar 3. Public Internet Access Programme-National Rural Internet Mission
- **CSCs–Made Viable, Multi-functional End-points for Service Delivery**
A. Coverage: 2,50,000 villages (now 1,30,000).
B. Timeline: 3 Years-March 2017.
C. Cost: ₹ 4,750 crore.
D. Nodal Agency: DeitY.
- **Post Offices to become Multi-Service Centres**
A. Coverage: 1,50,000 post offices.
B. Timeline: 2 Years.
C. Nodal Agency: D/o Posts.

D. Pillar 4: e-Governance: Reforming Government through Technology
- **Government Business Process Re-engineering Using IT to Improve Transactions**
A. Form simplification and reduction.

B. Online applications and tracking, and interface between departments.

C. Use of online repositories, e.g. school certificates, voter ID cards etc.

D. Integration of services and platforms—UIDAI, Payment Gateway, Mobile Platform, EDI.

- **Electronic Databases—All databases and information to be electronic, not manual.**
- **Workflow automation inside government.**
- **Public Grievance Redressal—Using IT to automate, respond, analyse data to identify and resolve persistent problems—largely process improvements.**

  E. Pillar 5: eKranti—Electronic Delivery of Services

- **Technology for Education—e-Education**

A. All schools connected with broadband.

B. Free wifi in all schools (2,50,000).

C. Digital literacy programme.

D. MOOCs (Massive Online Open Courses).

- **Technology for Health–e-Healthcare**

A. Online medical consultation.

B. Online medical records.

C. Online medicine supply.

D. Pan-India exchange for patient information.

E. Pilots–2015; Full coverage in 3 years.

- **Technology for Planning**

A. GIS based decision making.

B. National GIS Mission Mode Project.

- **Technology for Farmers**

A. Real time price information.

B. Online ordering of inputs.

C. Online cash, loan, relief payment with mobile banking.

- **Technology for Security**

A. Mobile emergency services.

- **Technology for Financial Inclusion**

A. Mobile banking.

B. Micro-ATM programme.

C. CSCs/Post Offices.
- **Technology for Justice**
A. e-Courts, e-Police, e- Jails, e-Prosecution.
- **Technology for Security**
A. National Cyber Security Co-ordination Centre.
   F. Pillar 6: Information for All
- **Online Hosting of Information and Documents**
A. Citizens have open, easy access to information.
B. Open data platform.
- **Government Pro-actively Engages through Social Media and Web-based Platforms to Inform Citizens**
A. MyGov.in.
B. 2-way communication between citizens and government.
- **Online Messaging to Citizens on Special Occasions and Programmes**
- **Largely Utilise Existing Infrastructure: Limited Additional Resources Needed**
   G. Pillar 7: Electronics Manufacturing: Target *Net Zero* **Imports by 2020**
- **Target** *Net Zero* **Imports is a Striking Demonstration of Intent**
- **Ambitious Goal which Requires Co-ordinated Action on Many Fronts**
A. Taxation, incentives.
B. Economies of scale, eliminate cost disadvantages.
C. Focused areas—big ticket items (FABS, Fab-less design, Set top boxes, VSATs, mobiles, consumer and medical electronics, smart energy meters, smart cards, micro-ATMs
D. Incubators, clusters.
E. Skill development.
F. Government procurement.
   H. Pillar 8: IT for Jobs
- **Train People in Smaller Towns and Villages for IT Sector Jobs**
A. Coverage: 1 crore students.
B. Timeline: 5 years.

C. Cost: ₹ 200 crore for weaker sections.
D. Nodal Agency: DeitY.
- **IT/ITES in North-East**
A. Scope: Setting up of BPO per NE State.
B. Coverage: NE States.
C. Nodal Agency: DeitY.
- **Train Service Delivery Agents to Run Viable Businesses Delivering IT Services**
A. Coverage: 3,00,000.
B. Timeline: 2 Years.
C. Nodal Agency: DeitY.
- **Telecom Service Providers to Train Rural Workforce to Cater to Their Own Needs**
A. Coverage: 5,00,000.
B. Timeline: 5 Years.
C. Nodal Agency: DoT.

I. Pillar 9: Early Harvest Programmes
- **IT Platform for Messages**
A. Coverage: Elected representatives, all Government employees.
B. 1.36 crore mobiles and 22 lakh e-mails.
C. Mass messaging application developed.
- **Government Greetings to be e-Greetings**
A. Basket of e-Greetings templates available.
B. Crowd sourcing of e-Greetings thru MyGov.
C. e-Greetings portal ready by August 14, 2014.
- **Biometric Attendance**
A. Coverage: All Central Government Offices in Delhi.
B. Operational in DeitY and initiated in urban development.
C. On-boarding started in other departments.
D. Procurement of devices–tender issued.
- **Wi-fi in All Universities**
A. Scope: All universities on NKN.
B. 400 additional Universities.
C. Cost: ₹ 790 crore.
- **Secure E-mail within Government**
A. Phase I upgradation for 10 lakh employees done.

B. Phase II for 50 lakh employees by March 2015.

C. Cost: ₹ 98 crore.

- **Standardize Government e-mail design**

A. Standardised templates under preparation.

- **Public Wi-fi Hotspots**

A. Coverage: Cities with population >1 million, tourist centres.

B. Nodal Agency: DoT/MoUD.

- **School Books to be e-Books**

A. Nodal Agency: MHRD/DeitY.

- **SMS-based Weather Information, Disaster Alerts**

A. DeitY's Mobile Seva Platform ready.

B. Nodal Agency: MoES (IMD)/MHA (NDMA).

- **National Portal for Lost and Found Children**

A. Nodal Agency: DeitY/DoWCD.

4.3.4 Estimated Cost

- **Overall Costs of Digital India**

~ ₹ 1,00,000 crore in ongoing schemes.

~ ₹ 13,000 crore for new schemes and activities.

4.3.5 Impact of Digital India by 2019

- Broadband in 2.5 lakh villages, and universal phone connectivity.
- Net Zero Imports by 2020.
- 4,00,000 Public Internet Access Points.
- Wi-fi in 2.5 lakh schools, all universities; Public wi-fi hotspots for citizens.
- Digital Inclusion: 1.7 crore trained for IT, telecom and electronics jobs.
- Job creation: Direct 1.7 crore and Indirect at least 8.5 crore.
- e-Governance and e-Services: Across Government.
- India to be leader in IT use in services—health, education, banking.
- Digitally-empowered citizens—public cloud, internet access.

4.3.6 Challenges and Changes Needed

- Programme on this scale never conceived.

- Each pillar/programme has own challenges.
- Human resource issues.
A. NIC-not equipped for a fraction of this task (obsolesce)— needs revamping and restructuring.
B. DeitY—needs programme managers—at least 4 more officers at senior levels.
C. Ministries—need a chief information officer/chief technology officer.
- **Financial Resources Issues**
A. Mostly structured around ongoing programmes: Better focus, need some restructuring.
B. Some others are process improvements or better utilisation of resources.
C. A few new programmes may be needed, particularly in electronics manufacturing and skill development.
- **Co-ordination Issues**
A. Programme covers many other departments.
B. Need commitment and effort.
C. Leadership and support critical for success.

4.3.7 Digital India (DI): A Critique: DI initiative is a promising initiative of the Indian Government. Many companies have shown their interest in this project. However, it is not free from challenges and legal hurdles. Some believe that DI cannot be successful till mandatory e-governance services are introduced in India. Incomplete implementation of the National e-Governance Plan of India will also adversely affect the success of the DI project. India has poor regulations in the field of privacy protection, data protection, cyber laws, telegraph, e-governance, e-commerce etc. Further, many legal experts believe that e-governance and DI without cyber security are useless. The cyber security trends in India have exposed the vulnerability of Indian cyberspace. Even the National Cyber Security Policy, 2013 has not been implemented till now. In these circumstances, critical infrastructure protection would be a tough task to manage for the Indian Government. The project also lacks the concept of proper e-waste management.

DI initiatives would be required to comply with the civil liberties requirements in general and civil liberties protection in cyberspace in particular. India has not given any importance to privacy and privacy laws so far. Indian Government indulges into mass surveillance in India and projects like Aadhaar, and Central Monitoring System are operating without any law and parliamentary oversight. The intelligence agencies of India like Intelligence Bureau (IB) and law enforcement agencies like Central Bureau of Investigation (CBI) are operating for decades without any law and parliamentary scrutiny. DI would further strengthen the mass surveillance activities of the Indian Government' if proper procedural safeguards are not implemented and practiced.

The initiative is commendable and deserves full support of all stakeholders. Nevertheless, the initiative lacks some crucial components including inadequate legal framework, absence of privacy and data protection laws, possibilities of civil liberties abuse, lack of parliamentary oversight for e-surveillance, lack of intelligence-related reforms, insecure Indian cyberspace etc. These issues have to be addressed for successful planning and implementation of DI initiative. Still, DI project is worth exploring and implementation despite its shortcomings that can be rectified before/during its implementation.

If correctly implemented, Digital India project can change the way public services would be delivered in India in the near future.

5

Governance with Digital Tools

IT is the world's fastest growing economic activity. It is transforming resource-based economies to knowledge-based economies. IT has become the greatest agent of change and promises to play this role even more dramatically in future. IT changes every aspect of human life, apart from impacting changes in the field of communications, trade, manufacturing, services, culture, entertainment, education, research and national security. IT has broken old barriers and is building new interconnections in the emerging concept of a single global village. It has also become one of the critical indicators of the progress of nations, communities and individuals.

The advent of IT offers opportunities to overcome historical disabilities. IT is a tool that will enable nations to achieve the goal of becoming a strong, prosperous and self-confident state. IT promises to compress the time it would otherwise take for countries to advance rapidly in their march towards faster development.

5.1 Governance: Theoretical Framework

In its most abstract sense, governance is a theoretical concept referring to the actions and processes by which stable practices and organizations arise and persist. These actions and processes may operate in formal and informal organizations of any size; and they may function for any purpose, good or evil, for profit or not. Conceiving of governance in this way, one can apply the concept to states, to corporations, to non-profits, to NGOs, to partnerships and other associations, to project teams, and to any number of humans engaged in some purposeful activity.

Most theories of governance as process arose out of neoclassical economics. These theories build deductive models, based on the assumptions of modern economics, to show how rational actors may come to establish and sustain formal organizations, including firms and states, and informal organizations, such as networks and practices for governing the commons. Many of these theories draw on transaction cost economics

5.1.1 Governance Defined: Governance is a very general concept that can refer to all manner of entities. Equally, this generality means that governance is often defined more narrowly to refer to a particular *level* of governance associated with a type of organization (including public governance, global governance, non-profit governance, corporate governance, and project governance), a particular *field* of governance associated with a type of activity or outcome (including environmental governance, internet governance, and information technology governance), or a particular *model* of governance, often derived as an empirical or normative theory (including regulatory governance, participatory governance, multi-level governance, meta-governance, and collaborative governance). Governance can be used not only to describe these diverse topics but also to define normative or practical agendas for them.

Normative concepts of fair governance or good governance are common among political, public sector, voluntary, and private sector organizations.

The World Bank defines governance as "the manner in which power is exercised in the management of a country's economic and social resources for development". The Worldwide Governance Indicators project of the World Bank defines governance as "the traditions and institutions by which authority in a country is exercised."

According to the United Nations Development Programme's Regional Project on Local Governance for Latin America, "Governance has been defined as the rules of the political system to solve conflicts between actors and adopt decision (legality). It has also been used to describe the "proper functioning of institutions and their acceptance by the public". And it has been used to invoke the efficacy of government and the achievement of consensus by democratic means.

Governance refers to "all of processes of governing, whether undertaken by a government, market or network, whether over a family, tribe, formal or informal organization or territory and whether through the laws, norms, power or language". It relates to "the processes of interaction and decision-making among the actors involved in a collective problem that lead to the creation, reinforcement, or reproduction of social norms and institutions".

5.1.2 Importance of Governance: Better governance is crucial for translating the large development and welfare expenditure of the public authorities into enduring outcomes on the ground. While there is general appreciation that development programmes have the right objectives, their implementation on the ground is poor. Implementation of programmes can be improved through a multi-faceted approach relying on professionalization of public service delivery, total quality management (TQM), innovative use of digital and other technologies which improve monitoring and supervision. It can also be improved through: (a) greater emphasis on social mobilisation and capacity building, (b) strengthening of local institutions, and (c) building deeper partnerships with civil society organisations and the community to determine the needs and aspirations of the people.

Implementation in many areas—particularly in infrastructure development involving large projects—is held up for a variety of reasons. Co-ordination needed across different agencies to facilitate progress in project implementation is often lacking and can lead to long delays and cost over-runs. Project management capabilities must be improved for the country to get better returns from public investment in infrastructure and also in the social sectors.

Corruption distorts the decision-making mechanism and leads to an inefficient distribution of resources. Improving anti-corruption efforts is one of the highest rated priorities of the business leaders. India should work closely with the relevant international organizations and give particular importance to the fight against corruption in the public and private sectors. Measures to increase transparency in government-business relations will have a corrective impact on corruption.

A number of initiatives need to be urgently pursued to rid the system of corruption, which is both morally abhorrent and imposes economic costs. Several legislative measures are needed. These include the establishment of an effective Lokpal, introduction of a law on public procurement and transparency, and the creation of a legislative framework governing the functioning of regulatory institutions so as to ensure both functional autonomy and accountability.

To combat corruption, it is imperative to ensure speedy prosecution and trial in corruption cases. The long delays in the judicial process are an important factor behind the growing cynicism about the rule of law in our system. Reforms in the legal process need to be put in place without further delays.

The use of information technology (IT)—world's fastest growing economic activity—to improve governance cannot be over-emphasized. It is transforming resource-based economies to knowledge-based economies. IT has become the greatest agent of change and promises to play this role even more dramatically in future. IT changes every aspect of human life, apart from impacting changes in the field of communications, trade, manufacturing, services, culture, entertainment, education, research and national security. IT has broken old barriers and is building new interconnections in the emerging concept of a single global village. It has also become one of the critical indicators of the progress of nations, communities and individuals.

The advent of IT offers opportunities to overcome historical disabilities. IT is a tool that will enable nations to achieve the goal of becoming a strong, prosperous and self-confident state. IT promises to compress the time it would otherwise take for countries to advance rapidly in their march towards faster development.

5.1.3 Three Broad Dimensions of Governance: A variety of entities (known generically as *governing bodies*) can govern. The most formal is a *government*, a body whose sole responsibility and authority is to make binding decisions in a given geo-political system (such as a state) by establishing laws. Other types of governing bodies are possible. These include an organization (such as a corporation recognized as a legal entity by a government), a socio-political group (chiefdom, tribe, family, religious denomination, etc.), or another, informal group of people.

Whatever form the entity takes, its *governance* is the way the rules, norms and actions are produced, sustained, regulated and held accountable. The degree of formality depends on the internal rules of a given organization. As such, governance may take many forms, driven by many different motivations and with many different results. For instance, a government may operate as a democracy where citizens vote on who should govern and the public good is the goal, while a non-profit organization may be governed by a small board of directors and pursue more specific aims.

In addition, a variety of external actors without decision-making power can influence the process of governing. These include lobbies, political parties, and the media.

A. Public Governance: It is useful to note the distinction between the concepts of governance and politics. Politics involves processes by which a group of people (perhaps with divergent opinions or interests) reach collective decisions generally regarded as binding on the group, and enforced as common policy. Governance, on the other hand, conveys the administrative and process-oriented elements of governing rather than its antagonistic ones. Such an argument continues to assume the possibility of the traditional separation between *politics* and *administration*. Contemporary governance practice and theory sometimes questions this distinction, premising that both *governance* and *politics* involve aspects of power and accountability.

In general terms, public governance occurs in three broad ways:

- Through networks of public-private-partnerships (PPPs) or with the collaboration of community organisations.
- Through the use of market mechanisms whereby market principles of competition serve to allocate resources while operating under government regulation.
- Through top-down methods that primarily involve governments and the state bureaucracy.

B. Private Governance: Private governance occurs when non-governmental entities—like private organizations, dispute resolution bodies, or other third party groups—make rules and/or standards which have a binding effect on the quality of life and opportunities of the larger public. Simply put, private—not public—entities are making public policy. For example, insurance companies exert a great societal impact, largely invisible and freely accepted, that is a private form of governance in society. In turn, reinsurers, as private companies, may exert similar private governance over their underlying carriers. The term *public policy* should not be exclusively associated with policy that is made by government. Public policy may be created by either the private sector or the public sector. If one wishes to refer only to public policy that is made by government, the best term to use is *governmental policy*, which eliminates the ambiguity regarding the agent of the policy making.

C. Global Governance: Global governance is defined as the complex of formal and informal institutions, mechanisms, relationships, and processes between and among states, markets, citizens and organizations, both inter- and non-governmental, through which collective interests on the global plane are articulated, right and obligations are established, and differences are mediated. In short, global governance denotes the regulation of interdependent relations in the absence of an overarching political authority. The best example of this is the international system or relationships between independent states. The term, however, can apply wherever a group of free equals needs to form a regular relationship.

5.1.4 Forms of Governance: These are as under:

A. Non-profit Governance: Non-profit governance has a dual focus: achieving the organization's social mission and ensuring that organization is viabile. Both responsibilities relate to fiduciary responsibility that a board of trustees has with respect to the exercise of authority over the explicit actions the organization takes. Public trust and accountability is an essential aspect of organizational viability so it achieves the social mission in a way that is respected by those whom the organization serves and the society in which it is located.

B. Corporate Governance: Corporate organizations often use the word *governance* to describe both:

- The manner in which boards or their likes direct a corporation.
- The laws and customs (rules) applying to that direction.

Corporate governance consists of the set of processes, customs, policies, laws and institutions affecting the way people direct, administer or control a corporation. Corporate governance also includes the relationships among the many players involved (the stakeholders) and the corporate goals. The principal players include the shareholders, management, and the board of directors. Other stakeholders include employees, suppliers, customers, banks and other lenders, regulators, the environment and the community at large.

C. Regulatory Governance: Regulatory governance reflects the emergence of decentred and mutually adaptive policy regimes which rests on regulation rather than service provision or taxing and spending. The term captures the tendency of policy regimes to deal with complexity with delegated system of rules. It is likely to appear in arenas and nations which are more complex, more global, more contested and more liberally democratic. The term builds upon and extends the terms of the regulatory state on the one hand and governance on the other. While the term regulatory state marginalize non-state actors (NGOs etc.) in the domestic and global level, the term governance marginalizes regulation as a constitutive instrument of governance. The term regulatory governance, therefore, refers to governance beyond the state and governance via regulation.

D. Participatory Governance: Participatory governance focuses on deepening democratic engagement through the participation of citizens in the processes of governance with the state. The idea is that citizens should play a more direct role in public decision-making or at least engage more deeply with political issues. Government officials should also be responsive to this kind of engagement. In practice, participatory governance can supplement the roles of citizens as voters or as watchdogs through more direct forms of involvement.

E. Meta-governance: Meta-governance is widely defined as the *governing of governing.* It represents the established ethical principles, or *norms,* that shape and steer the entire governing process. It is important to note that there are no clearly defined settings within which meta-governing takes place, or particular persons who are responsible for it. While some believe meta-governing to be the role of the state which is assumed to steer actors in a particular direction, it can potentially be exercised by any resourceful actor who wishes to influence the governing process. Examples of this include the publishing of codes of conduct at the highest level of international government, and media focus on specific issues at the socio-cultural level. Despite their different sources, both seek to establish values in such a way that they become accepted *norms.* The fact that *norms* can be established at any level and can then be used to shape the governance process as a whole, means meta-governance is part of both the input and the output of the governing system.

F. Fair Governance: When discussing governance in particular organisations, the quality of governance within the organisation is often compared to a standard of good governance.

In the case of a business or of a non-profit organization, for example, good governance relates to consistent management, cohesive policies, guidance, processes and decision-rights for a given area of responsibility, and proper oversight and accountability.

G. Good Governance: Good governance implies that mechanisms function in a way that allows the executives to respect the rights and interests of the stakeholders, in a spirit of democracy. Good governance is an indeterminate term used in international development literature to describe various normative accounts of how public institutions ought to conduct public affairs and manage public resources. These normative accounts are often justified on the grounds that they are thought to be conducive to economic ends, such as the eradication of poverty and successful economic development. Unsurprisingly different organizations have defined governance and good governance differently to promote different normative ends.

5.1.5 Measuring Governance: Several efforts have been made to assess and measure the quality of governance of countries all around the world.

In recent years, measuring governance is inherently a controversial and political exercise. A distinction is, therefore, made between external assessments, peer assessments and self-assessments.

Examples of external assessments are donor assessments or comparative indices produced by international non-governmental organisations. An example of a peer assessment is the African Peer Review Mechanism. Examples of self-assessments are country-led assessments that can be led by government, civil society, researchers and/or other stakeholders at the national level.

One of these efforts to create an internationally comparable measure of governance—and an example of an external assessment—is the Worldwide Governance Indicators project, developed by members of the World Bank and the World Bank Institute. The project reports aggregate and individual indicators for more than 200 countries for 6 dimensions of governance:

1. Voice and accountability.
2. Political stability and lack of violence.
3. Government effectiveness.
4. Regulatory quality.
5. Rule of law.
6. Control of corruption.

To complement the macro-level cross-country Worldwide Governance Indicators, the World Bank Institute developed the World Bank Governance Surveys, which are country-level governance assessment tools that operate at the micro or sub-national level and use information gathered from a country's own citizens, business people and public sector workers to diagnose governance vulnerabilities and suggest concrete approaches for fighting corruption.

A new Worldwide Governance Index (WGI) has been developed and is open for improvement through public participation. The following domains, in the form of indicators and composite indexes, were selected to achieve the development of the WGI:
1. Peace and security.
2. Rule of law.
3. Human rights and participation.
4. Sustainable development.
5. Human development.

Additionally, in 2009 the Bertelsmann Foundation published the Sustainable Governance Indicators (SGI), which systematically measure the need for reform and the capacity for reform within the Organisation for Economic Co-operation and Development (OECD) countries. The project examines to what extent governments can identify, formulate and implement effective reforms that render a society well-equipped to meet future challenges, and ensure their future viability.

A. Governance Analytical Framework (GAF): GAF is a practical methodology for investigating governance processes, where various stakeholders interact and make decisions regarding collective issues, thus creating or reinforcing social norms and institutions. It is postulated that governance processes can be found in any society, and unlike other approaches, that these can be observed and analysed from a non-normative perspective. It proposes a methodology based on five main analytical units: problems, actors, norms, processes and nodal points. These logically articulated analytical units make up a coherent methodology aimed at being used as a tool for empirical social policy research.

5.2 Digital Tools for Improving Public Services in India

A number of services are today provided by the Central and State Governments. These include ration cards, caste certificates, income certificates, certificates for proof of residence, passports and similar other services. It is important that these are available within a prescribed time line. Failures and deficiencies in delivery of public services lead to dissatisfaction and public anger against the government. Various government agencies have taken initiatives to notify services and time-limits within which these are to be availed of. An important aid to delivery of services can be the use of e-governance and technology. The use of technology in delivery of public services will need to be expanded rapidly to reduce delays and discretion used to the advantage of the citizen.

5.2.1 Unique Identification (UID) System: In a citizen-centric system of governance, the citizen's satisfaction becomes the measure of success of both service delivery as well as programme delivery. A citizen's identity, therefore, becomes important both in developmental as well as regulatory administration. The absence of a reliable system for such purposes has been an impediment to improving targeting of developmental schemes and reducing leakages in the delivery system.

Many major individual-oriented Government programmes incorporate a provision for collection of information at the individual/family level. In most cases, this is undertaken as a de novo exercise without reference to similar exercises undertaken in the past by other government departments and sometimes even by the same department. The absence of a system of updation of such purpose-specific databases and the lack of a system for corroboration among such departments are also factors leading inevitably to expensive, time consuming and error-prone de novo surveys for data collection for each scheme. To create a common platform for service/programme delivery, UID system has been introduced in India.

Development of unique ID numbers with biometrics to establish proof of identity is an important area which has been thrown open for use of technology. This would help in providing services to various users and result in controlling fake cards and thereby bring enormous savings. The financial inclusion services are also feasible by using UID and the telecom services. It is also possible to use technology for expanding banking correspondence and thereby expand the extent of banking services.

UID System is envisioned as a means for residents to easily establish their identity, anywhere in the country. It is an important step towards ensuring that residents in India can access the resources and benefits they are entitled to. A resident can enrol for a UID number by providing basic demographic as well as biometric details to the enrolling agency. The enrolling agency will transmit these details to a central UID server. The server will then perform a de-duplication check using the resident's key demographic and biometric fields against existing UID records in the database, to ensure that he/she does not already have a UID number.

Once the check confirms that a duplicate record does not exist, the central system will issue a UID number to the resident. The resident can then use the number with different service providers, who can verify his or her identity online. The agency has to transmit the UID number and information provided by the resident to the UID server, and the server immediately responds with a yes or a no.

UID can have a significant impact on service delivery. The existing patchwork of multiple agency databases in India gives individuals the incentive to provide different personal information to different agencies and also impersonate someone else. In the UID infrastructure, all resident records are stored in a central database, and each new entry is de-duplicated. Consequently, residents can only have one UID number, which is mobile and can be used anywhere in the country. The lack of duplicates, and accuracy and mobility in identity verification, reduces opportunities for fraud and enables agencies across the country to provide residents with targeted, effective services and benefits.

5.2.2 Smart Cards: The UID Project will eventually become the underpinning of the Citizens Smart Card Project of the Ministry of Home Affairs—both are aimed at identifying citizens, providing them a unique identity and in case of the MHA project, also will provide a Smart Card which has all this information.

The smart card would have a memory partitioned into distinct modules representing different entitlement groups for which free services or implicit/explicit subsidies are given. These include food and nutrition, energy (kerosene, LPG, electricity), education services, health services, civic amenities and services (drinking water, latrines/sanitation), employment and farming (fertilizer, irrigation etc.).

Any subsidy received by any individual would be entered on his/her smart card when the goods or service is delivered/charged for by the authorized supplier (for example, the fair price shop, kerosene/LPG dealer, fertilizer outlet). The rules and regulations for delivery of subsidy and its reimbursement to the goods/service supplier would be defined by the concerned department.

The data entered on the smart card would be accessible by all monitoring/evaluating agencies so that they can put together a picture of what subsidies are being received by whom, as well as those who are not receiving a subsidy for which they are eligible.

5.2.3 National e-Governance Plan (NeGP): Government

approved the National e-Governance Plan (NeGP) in May 2006 with the following vision: 'Make all Government services accessible to the common man in his locality, through common service delivery outlets and ensure efficiency, transparency and reliability of such services at affordable costs to realize the basic needs of the common man'. One major difference from the computerization initiatives of the past is the focus on delivery of services to citizens.

The architecture for e-Governance envisaged in NeGP aims to leverage e-Governance optimally to radically change the way government delivers services to citizens; addresses developmental challenges in key areas like education, health and agriculture; implements major programmes; and even the way it conducts its own business. In fact, key governance objectives like citizen centricity, transparency and efficiency cannot be achieved without extensive and pervasive use of technology.

NeGP seeks to lay the foundation and provide impetus for the long-term growth of e-Governance in the country. It also seeks to create the right governance and institutional mechanisms, lay down appropriate policies and set up the core infrastructure, all of which would facilitate implementation of various programmes and projects of the government. A body under the Chairpersonship of the Prime Minister has been constituted to prescribe deliverables and milestones, and monitor periodically the implementation of NeGP.

5.3 Digital Tools for Tax Administration

Central Board of Direct Taxes (CBDT), New Delhi, is part of the Department of Revenue in the Ministry of Finance. While the CBDT provides essential inputs for policy and planning of direct taxes in India, it is also responsible for administration of direct tax laws through its Income Tax Department. The Income Tax Department is primarily responsible for combating the menace of black money. For this purpose, it uses the tools of scrutiny assessment as well as information-based investigations for detecting tax evasion and penalizing the same as per provisions of the Income Tax Act, 1961 with the objective of creating deterrence against tax evasion. In doing so, it plays one of the most important roles in preventing generation, accumulation, and consumption of unaccounted black money. The Investigation Wing of the Income Tax Department deals with investigations to detect tax evasion and carries out operations like surveys and searches to collect evidence of such evasion. Such operations are usually carried out after detailed preliminary investigations and in cases involving substantial evasion of taxes.

The Income Tax Department is also engaged in the task of educating and assisting taxpayers in filing tax returns, assessing tax liability, demanding pending taxes, penalising dishonest taxpayers and disposing of tax disputes. The role of this Department in tax system of India is rapidly increasing as the share of direct taxes in the revenue of the country has registered a steady increase over the years.

5.3.1 E-filing of Returns: E-filing of income tax return is the process of electronically filing returns through internet which can be filed at any time at any place. While E-filing of income tax return is mandatory for a company and a firm liable to audit under Section 44AB, it is optional for other assessees. Similarly, Government has introduced e-filing of returns of tax deducted at source. It is mandatory for corporate deductors to furnish their TDS return in electronic form with effect from June 1, 2003. Further, it has been made mandatory for Government deductors and firms liable to audit under Section 44AB with effect from assessment year 2004-05. Deductors have to file e-TDS returns quarterly since assessment year 2005-06.

National Securities Depository Ltd. (NSDL) has been appointed as the e-TDS intermediary by the Income Tax Department. NSDL receives e-TDS returns from deductors on behalf of Income Tax Department. Deductors can submit e-TDS returns through TIN-Facilitation Centres established by NSDL or directly upload through NSDL website.

5.3.2 Online Tax Accounting System (OLTAS): Income

Tax Department operationalised OLTAS in July 2004. The new single copy challans have been introduced with effect from July 2005. The collecting bank branch will put a rubber stamp on the challan and its counter foil indicating a unique challan identification number (CIN), BSR code and challan serial number. The collecting bank has to capture the entire data of the challan and transmit it electronically to the Income Tax Department. The information received from banks is used by the Department to give credit for the tax paid based on CIN. This is a very significant step for creating tax information network.

To sum up, governance can be much more interactive if extensive use is made of all channels of communication including print and electronic media, social media, electronic boards in public places, written materials, website, an internet and other methods that have a wide reach and are able to convey messaging directly and swiftly.

India recognizes IT as the fastest and the most advanced vehicle of change for all-round progress and development of the country. In view of the potential of IT, the Government has advocated widespread proliferation of IT in the country and adopted various policy supports for promotion of IT in the fields of e-governance, empowerment of the people, education, industry, health, rural development, agriculture, and tourism.

5.3.3 Permanent Account Number (PAN): PAN issued by Income Tax Department is the critical element in capturing incomes and expenditures of a person. The Department identifies the assesses/persons with PAN which is a unique 10 digit alpha-numeric number. Obtaining PAN is compulsory not only for income tax purposes but also for certain other purposes/transactions. PAN is to be obtained only once for ever. An assessee need not obtain a new PAN, even if he is transferred to any other place.

The Finance Act 1998 laid down that under Section 139-A a person whose taxable income is beyond basic exemption limit or turnover exceeds ₹ 5 lakh is required to apply for PAN. Every person has to quote PAN on any document while dealing with Income Tax Department and financial transactions exceeding the specified limit. It has been made compulsory for tax deductors to quote PAN of the deductees in the return of tax deducted and certificate issued to the deductees with effect from June 1, 2001. The Finance Act, 2009 provided that if PAN is not quoted by the deductee, the TDS rate will be 20 percent instead of 10 percent. The main purpose of these amendments has been to compel people to quote PAN, so that information contained in such returns or certificates can be processed properly.

5.3.4 Digital Signature: A person desiring to furnish his return of income electronically, may sign it digitally or manually. For signing the return digitally, he is required to obtain a digital signature. A digital signature is the electronic signature issued by the certifying authority that shows the authenticity of the person signing the same.

5.3.5 Goods and Service Tax Network (GSTN): Among the various steps that are being taken for the introduction of goods and services tax (GST) is the establishment of a strong information technology (IT) infrastructure. For this purpose, the Government has set up an Empowered Group (Chairman: Nandan Nilekani). Significant progress has been made in the conceptualization and design of the GSTN—a common portal for the Centre and States that will enable electronic processing of the key business processes of registration, returns, and payments.

For the implementation of GST in the country, the Central and State Governments have jointly registered GSTN as a not-for-profit, non-government company under Section 25 of the Companies Act, 1956. It will provide shared IT infrastructure and services to Central and State Governments, tax payers and other stakeholders. GSTN is a special purpose vehicle (SPV) which aims to provide a standard and uniform interface to the taxpayers, and shared infrastructure and services to Central and State/UT Governments. It will be the interface between the government and the taxpayers.

GSTN is working on developing a state-of-the-art comprehensive IT infrastructure including the common GST portal providing front-end services of registration, payments and returns to taxpayers. It will also assist some States with back-end IT modules that include processing of returns, registrations, audits, assessments, appeals, etc. All States, accounting authorities, Reserve Bank of India (RBI) and banks are also preparing their IT infrastructure for the administration of GST. There would be no manual filing of returns. All taxes can also be paid online. All mis-matched returns would be auto-generated, and there would be no need for manual interventions. Most returns would be self-assessed.

The functions of the GSTN, inter alia, include the following:

1. Facilitating registration.
2. Forwarding the returns to Central and State authorities.
3. Computation and settlement of IGST.
4. Matching of tax payment details with banking network.
5. Providing various MIS reports to the Central and the State Governments based on the tax payer return information.
6. Providing analysis of tax payers' profile.
7. Running the matching engine for matching, reversal and reclaim of input tax credit.

GSTN would also be integrating the common GST portal with the existing tax administration IT systems and would be building interfaces for taxpayers.

GSTN is a unique and complex IT initiative. It is unique as it seeks, for the first time, to establish a uniform interface for the taxpayer and a common and shared IT infrastructure between the Centre and States. Currently, the Centre and State indirect tax administrations work under different laws, regulations, procedures and formats and consequently the IT systems work as independent sites. Integrating them for GST implementation would be complex since it would involve integrating the entire indirect tax ecosystem so as to bring all the tax administrations (Centre, State and Union Territories) to the same level of IT maturity with uniform formats and interfaces for taxpayers and other external stakeholders. Besides, GST being a destination-based tax, the inter-state trade of goods and services would need a robust settlement mechanism amongst the States and the Centre. This is possible only when there is a strong IT infrastructure and service backbone which enables to capture, process and exchange information amongst the stakeholders.

GSTN will render the following services through the common GST Portal:

1. Registration (including existing taxpayer master migration and issue of PAN-based registration number).
2. Payment management including payment gateways and integration with banking systems.
3. Return filing and processing.
4. Taxpayer management, including account management, notifications, information, and status tracking.
5. Tax authority account and ledger management.
6. Computation of settlement (including IGST settlement) between the Centre and States; clearing house for IGST.
7. Processing and reconciliation of GST on imports and integration with EDI systems of Customs.
8. MIS including need-based information and business intelligence.
9. Maintenance of interfaces between the Common GST Portal and tax administration systems.
10. Providing training to stakeholders.
11. Providing analytics and business intelligence to tax authorities.
12. Carrying out research, study best practices and provide training to stakeholders.

The structure of GSTN has been approved by the EC. GSTN will be set up as a National Information Utility. GSTN will implement common PAN-based registration, returns filing and payments processing for all States on a shared platform. The use of PAN as a common identifier in both direct and indirect taxes, will enhance transparency and check tax evasion.

National Securities Depository Limited (NSDL) has been selected as technology partner for incubating the National Information Utility that will establish and operate the IT backbone for the GST. In this regard, NSDL has set up a pilot project in collaboration with 11 States prior to GST roll-out across the country. Three Joint Working Groups of officials have also been constituted comprising officials from the Central Government, State Governments, and the Empowered Committee (EC) of State Finance Ministers to work on legislation, business procedures and IT infrastructure respectively.

GSTN has already appointed M/s Infosys as Managed Service Provider.

6

Internet Banking and Mobile Banking

Digital technology has transformed the functioning of businesses, the world over. It has: (a) bridged the gaps in terms of the reach and the coverage of systems (b) enabled better decision-making based on latest and accurate information, (c) reduced costs and (d) improved overall improvement in efficiency. In the Indian context, the financial sector, especially the banking sector, has been a major beneficiary from the inroads made by IT.

Many new processes, products and services offered by banks and other financial intermediaries are now IT-centred. Banks have traditionally been in the forefront of harnessing technology to improve their products, services and efficiency. They have, over a long time, been using electronic and telecommunication networks for delivering a wide range of value added products and services. The delivery channels include, inter alia, direct dial-up connections, private networks, public networks and the devices including telephone, personal computers (PCs), automated teller machines (ATMs), networking of ATMs in the form of shared payment networks, and core banking solutions.

With the popularity of PCs, easy access to internet and world wide web (www), internet is increasingly used by banks as a channel for receiving instructions and delivering their products and services to their customers. This form of banking is generally referred to as internet banking, although the range of products and services offered by different banks vary widely both in their content and sophistication.

6.1 Internet Banking

6.1.1 Internet Banking and Electronic Banking (E-banking): E-banking) is a generic term encompassing internet banking, telephone banking, mobile banking etc. In other words, it is a process of delivery of banking' services and products through electronic channels such as satellite, telephone, internet, cell phone etc. The concept and scope of e-banking is still evolving. Internet banking is a major component of e-banking.

Internet banking offers different online services like balance enquiry, requests for cheque books, recording stop-payment instructions, balance transfer instructions, account opening and other forms of traditional banking services. These are mostly traditional services offered through internet as a new delivery channel. Banks are also offering payment services on behalf of their customers who shop in different e-shops, e-malls etc.

6.1.2 Levels of Banking Services Offered through Internet: Internet banking applications run on diverse platforms and operating systems and use different architectures. The product may support centralized (bank-wide) operations or branch level automation. It may have a distributed, client server or three-tier architecture based on a file system. Moreover, the product may run on computer systems of various types ranging from PCs, open (Unix based) systems, to proprietary main frames. These products allow different levels of access to the customers and different range of facilities. The products accessible through Internet can be classified into three types based on the levels of access granted.

A. Basic Level Services (or Information Only Systems): These refer to websites of banks which disseminate information on different products and services offered to customers and members of public in general. A bank may receive and reply to queries of customers through e-mail. General purpose information like interest rates, branch locations, product features, loan and deposit calculators are provided on the website of a bank. The sites also allow downloading of application forms. Interactivity is limited to a simple form of e-mail. No identification or authentication of customers is done and there is no interaction between the bank's production system (where current data of accounts are kept and transactions are processed) and the customer.

B. Simple Transactional Systems: These allow customers to submit their instructions, applications for different services, queries on their account balances etc., but do not permit any fund-based transactions on their accounts. These systems provide customer-specific information in the form of account balances, transaction details, statement of account etc. The information is still largely *read only*. Identification and authentication of customer takes place using relatively simple techniques (like passwords). Information is fetched from the production system of the bank in either the batch mode or offline. Thus, the main application system of the bank is not directly accessed.

C. Fully Transactional Websites: These websites allow the customers to operate on their accounts for transfer of funds, payment of different bills, subscribing to other products of the bank and to transact purchase and sale of securities etc. These systems provide bi-directional transaction capabilities. The bank allows customers to submit transactions on its systems and these directly update customers' accounts. Therefore, security and control system need to be strongest here.

The above forms of internet banking services are offered by traditional banks as an additional method of serving the customer or by new banks who deliver banking services primarily through internet or other electronic delivery channels as the value added services. Some of these banks are known as *virtual banks* or *internet-only-banks* (IOBs) and may not have any physical presence in a country despite offering different banking services. Thus, internet banking is nothing more than traditional banking services delivered through an electronic communication backbone, viz. internet. However, in the process it has thrown open issues which have ramifications beyond what a new delivery channel would normally envisage. Hence, it has compelled regulators world over to take note of this emerging channel.

6.1.3 Security Risks: Security in internet banking comprises both the computer and communication security. The aim of computer security is to preserve computing resources against abuse and unauthorized use, and to protect data from accidental and deliberate damage, disclosure and modification. The communication security aims to protect data during the transmission in computer network and distributed system.

External threats such as *hacking* [1], *sniffing* [2], *spoofing* [3] and *denial of service* [4] attacks expose banks to new security risks. Open electronic delivery channels create new security issues for banks with respect to confidentiality and integrity of information, non-repudiation of transactions, authentication of users and access control.

When a bank's system is connected to the internet, an attack could originate at any time from anywhere. Some acceptable level of security must be established before business on the internet can be reliably conducted. Following are some familiar forms of attacks:

1. An intruder gains unauthorized access and nothing more.
2. An intruder gains access and destroys, corrupts or otherwise alters data.
3. An intruder gains access and seizes control partly or wholly, perhaps denying access to privileged users.
4. An intruder does not gain access, but instead forges messages from your system.
5. An intruder does not gain access, but instead implements malicious procedures that cause the network to fail, reboot, and hang.

Modern security techniques have made cracking very difficult but not impossible. Further more, if the system is not configured properly or the updated patches are not installed then hackers may crack the system using security hole. A wide range of information regarding security hole and their fixes is freely available on the internet. System administrators should keep themselves updated with this information.

Most banks appear to be sensitive to external security threats.

Among the issues identified for immediate attention is the development of more robust tools to verify the identity and authenticity of larger value transaction requests. [5] In addition, the banking industry needs to continue to work towards international best practices for encryption requirements, including the legality of electronic signature and records. Moreover, since many banks' internal networks rely on security technology similar to that used to manage their external systems, it is important that bankers also be sensitive to managing the security risk arising from their internal networks. If not managed properly, internal security exposures can also compromise the integrity and confidentiality of bank records and customer data. [6]

6.1.4 Internet Banking in India: Internet banking—both as a medium of delivery of banking services and as a strategic tool for business development—has gained wide acceptance internationally and is fast catching up in India with more and more banks entering the fray. India can be said to be on the threshold of a major banking revolution with net banking having already been unveiled.

The growth potential of internet banking in India is immense. Further incentives provided by banks would dissuade customers from visiting physical branches, and thus get 'hooked' to the convenience of arm-chair banking. The facility of accessing their accounts from anywhere in the world by using a home computer with Internet connection, is particularly fascinating to non-resident Indians and high net worth individuals having multiple bank accounts.

Costs of banking service through the internet form a fraction of costs through conventional methods. The cost conscious banks in the country have therefore actively considered use of internet as a channel for providing services. Fully computerized banks, with better management of their customer base are in a stronger position to cross-sell their products through this channel.

A. Products and Services Offered: Banks in India are at different stages of the web-enabled banking cycle. Initially, a bank, which is not having a website, allows its customer to communicate with it through an e-mail address; communication is limited to a small number of branches and offices which have access to this e-mail account. As yet, many scheduled commercial banks in India are still in the first stage of internet banking operations.

With gradual adoption of information technology, the bank puts up a website that provides general information on the banks, its location, services available e.g. loan and deposits products, application forms for downloading and e-mail option for enquiries and feedback. It is largely a marketing or an advertising tool. Customers are required to fill in applications on the internet and can later receive loans or other products requested for at their local branch. A few banks provide the customer to enquire into his demat account (securities/shares) holding details, transaction details and status of instructions given by him.

Some of the banks permit customers to interact with them and transact electronically with them. Such services include request for opening of accounts, requisition for cheque books, stop payment of cheques, viewing and printing statements of accounts, movement of funds between accounts within the same bank, querying on status of requests, instructions for opening of letters of credit and bank guarantees etc.

Banks are thus looking to position themselves as one-stop financial shops. Some banks have tied up with computer training companies, computer manufacturers, internet services providers and portals for expanding their internet banking services, and widening their customer base. Setting up of internet kiosks and permeation through the cable television route to widen customer base are other priority areas in the agendas of the more aggressive players.

Banks providing internet banking services have been entering into agreements with their customers setting out the terms and conditions of the services. The terms and conditions include information on the access through user-id and secret password, minimum balance and charges, authority to the bank for carrying out transactions performed through the service, liability of the user and the bank, disclosure of personal information for statistical analysis and credit scoring also, non-transferability of the facility, notices and termination etc.

The race for market supremacy is compelling banks in India to adopt the latest technology on the internet in a bid to capture new markets and customers. Under mobile banking services, customers can scan their accounts to seek balance and payments status or instruct banks to issue cheques, pay bills or deliver statements of accounts.

Compared to banks abroad, Indian banks offering online services still have a long way to go. For online banking to reach a critical mass, there has to be sufficient number of users and the sufficient infrastructure in place. Though various security options like line encryption, branch connection encryption, firewalls, digital certificates, automatic sign-offs, random pop-ups and disaster recovery sites are in place or are being looked at, there is as yet no certification authority in India offering public key infrastructure which is absolutely necessary for online banking. The customer can only be assured of a secured conduit for its online activities if an authority certifying digital signatures is in place. The communication bandwidth presently available in India is also not enough to meet the needs of high priority services like online banking and trading. Banks offering online facilities need to have an effective disaster recovery plan along with comprehensive risk management measures. Banks offering online facilities also need to calculate their downtime losses, because even a few minutes of downtime in a week could mean substantial losses.

Some banks even today do not have uninterrupted power supply unit or systems to take care of prolonged power breakdown. Proper encryption of data and effective use of passwords are also matters that leave a lot to be desired. Systems and processes have to be put in place to ensure that errors do not take place.

Users of internet banking services are required to fill up

the application forms online and send a copy of the same by mail or fax to the bank. A contractual agreement is entered into by the customer with the bank for using the internet banking services. In this way, personal data in the applications forms is being held by the bank providing the service. The contract details are often one-sided, with the bank having the absolute discretion to amend or supplement any of the terms at any time. For these reasons domestic customers for whom other access points such as ATMs, telebanking, personal contact etc. are available, are often hesitant to use the internet banking services offered by Indian banks. Internet banking, as an additional delivery channel, may, therefore, be attractive and appealing as a value added service to domestic customers. Non-resident Indians for whom it is expensive and time consuming to access their bank accounts maintained in India find net banking very convenient and useful.

B. Information Technology Act, 2000: Government of India enacted The Information Technology Act, 2000, in order to provide legal recognition for transactions carried out by means of electronic data interchange and other means of electronic communication, commonly referred to as *electronic commerce*. The Act came into force with effect from October 17, 2000. The Act has also amended certain provisions of the Indian Penal Code, the Indian Evidence Act, 1872, The Bankers Book of Evidence Act, 1891 and Reserve Bank of India Act, 1934 in order to facilitate e-commerce in India. However, this Act does not apply to:

1. A negotiable instrument as defined in Section 13 of the Negotiable Instruments Act, 1881.
2. A power of attorney as defined in Section 1A of the Power of Attorney Act, 1882.
3. A trust as defined in Section 3 of the Indian Trusts Act, 1882.
4. A will as defined in clause (h) of Section 2 of the Indian Succession Act, 1925.
5. Any contract for the sale or conveyance of immovable

property or any interest in such property.

6. Any such class of documents or transactions as may be notified by the Central Government in the official Gazette.

Section 72 of the Information Technology Act, 2000 casts an obligation of confidentiality against disclosure of any electronic record, register, correspondence and information, except for certain purposes and violation of this provision is a criminal offence.

In the course of providing internet banking services the banks in India are facing new challenges relating to online opening of accounts, authentication, secrecy of customers accounts, non-repudiation, liability standards and consumer protection etc.

6.2 Mobile Banking

6.2.1 Introduction: Developments in mobile telephony, as also the mobile phone density in the India, present a unique opportunity to leverage the mobile platform to meet the objectives and challenges of financial inclusion. By harnessing the potential of mobile technology, large sections of the un-banked and under-banked society can be empowered to become inclusive through the use of electronic banking services.

The Payment and Settlement Systems (PSS) Act, 2007 empowers the Reserve Bank of India to authorize and regulate entities operating payment systems in the country. RBI has, over a period of time, placed importance on the move towards electronic payments and thereby a *less-cash* society. Towards this end, the RBI has been promoting and nurturing the growth of various modes of electronic payments including the pre-paid payment instruments, card payments, mobile banking etc.

The Payment Systems Vision Document 2012-15 of RBI, reflects the commitment towards provision of safe, efficient, accessible, inclusive, interoperable and authorised payment and settlement systems in the country. Recent experience shows that the share of paper-based instruments in the volume of total non-cash transactions has been declining in favour of electronic payments. In addition to the growth in volume as well as value processed by RTGS, the retail electronic segment too has registered a significant growth. Though overall volume of transactions in mobile banking is low, there has been significant growth in the volume recently.

6.2.2 Mobile Banking Regulatory Framework: In view of the potential of mobile as a channel for offering financial services in the country, RBI issued the first set of guidelines on mobile banking in October 2008. The mandate was that all transactions should originate from one bank account and terminate in another bank account. At this time, a few banks had already started offering information-based services like balance enquiry, stop payment instruction of cheques, transactions enquiry, location of the nearest ATM/branch etc. through this medium.

The guidelines issued by RBI in October 2008, permitted banks to facilitate funds transfer from one bank account to another bank account, both for personal remittances and purchase of goods and services. Banks were directed on the regulatory/supervisory issues, registration of customers for mobile banking, to ensure technology standards, interoperability, inter-bank clearing and settlement arrangements for fund transfers, customer grievance and redressal mechanism and transaction limits in an attempt to ensure safe, secure transfer of funds.

Under extant regulatory prescriptions, there is no monetary restriction on fund transfer effected through mobile banking as it is left to the risk perception of each bank and policies approved by their respective Boards. However, end-to-end encryption for transactions in excess of ₹ 5,000 has been mandated by RBI. Similarly, mobile as a channel for funds transfer from a bank account for cash payout to a beneficiary who does not have a bank account at ATMs/BCs—₹ 10,000 per transaction with a cap of ₹ 25,000 per beneficiary has also been permitted by RBI (under the Domestic Money Transfer Guidelines).

In line with these guidelines, banks have been offering mobile banking services to their customers through various channels such as SMS, USSD channel, mobile banking application etc. However, real time inter-bank mobile banking payments have been facilitated through the setting up of the inter-bank mobile payment services (IMPS), now termed as immediate payment service, and operated by the NPCI with the approval of RBI.

The IMPS has enhanced the efficiency of mobile banking by enabling real time transfer of funds between bank accounts and providing a centralised inter-bank settlement service for mobile banking transactions. The IMPS has also been enhanced to support merchant payments using mobile phones to promote less cash society.

Under the PSS Act, RBI has given permission for mobile banking services to 201 banks as on December 31, 2016. For the month of September 2016, the value of mobile banking transactions stood at ₹ 1042.57 billion.

6.2.3 Various Channels for Mobile Banking:

A. Mobile Banking: SMS-based Channel: SMS is a popular and widely used channel in mobile phones. It is ubiquitously available in all handsets irrespective of make and model and also GSM and CDMA enabled handsets. Most customers are very conversant with the SMS channel and use the same for various services including the short messaging. Many popular mobile VAS services such as cricket, jokes, horoscopes, etc. are based on SMS and used widely by customers.

Given the advantages offered by SMS channel, many banks have offered mobile banking services through the SMS channel. This includes non-financial services such as balance enquiry, mini statement, cheque book request, transaction alerts etc., and financial services such as funds transfer, mobile/DTH recharge, bill payments etc.

B. Mobile Banking: USSD-based Channel: Unstructured supplementary service data (USSD) is a protocol used by GSM cellular telephones to communicate with the telecom service provider's systems. USSD can be used for WAP browsing, pre-paid callback service, mobile-money services, location-based content services, menu-based information services, and as part of configuring the phone on the network.

USSD messages are up to 182 alphanumeric characters in length. Unlike short message service (SMS) messages, USSD messages create a real-time connection during a USSD session. The connection remains open, allowing a two-way exchange of a sequence of data. This makes USSD more interactive and advantageous than services that use SMS. USSD platform which is MNO dependent can be efficiently used by the mobile banking platforms. Realizing the benefits and potential of USSD-based mobile banking, some of the banks have launched USSD-based mobile banking services, e.g. State Bank of India, Canara Bank, ICICI Bank, with the help of telecom aggregators who in turn have tied up with few MNOs. For instance, ICICI Bank has tied up with Idea, Aircel, Tata Docomo, Reliance and MTNL for offering USSD platform to its customers on their GSM network.

C. Mobile Banking: Application based: All banks who have received the approval from RBI for mobile banking are offering the application-based mobile banking channel to their customers. Customers can download the mobile banking application and perform variety of services including the following: (a) Non-financial transactions such as balance enquiry, mini statement, cheque book request, (b) financial transactions such as funds transfer, mobile/DTH recharge, bill payments etc.

The mobile application is offered on various platforms such as Java, Symbian, Blackberry OS, Windows, Android, Apple iOS etc. Many Banks have made the mobile application available in the app stores such as Google, Apple, Blackberry, etc. for easy search and download by the customers.

Following are the advantages of the application-based mobile banking:

- Applications once downloaded are easy to use for the customers who are proficient in using the smart phone based applications.
- Banks have made these applications compliant with most of the latest operating systems covering the large range of smart

phones in use.

- It has been experienced by the banks that once customer has used the application-based mobile banking, he continues to use the same unless there is a change of the handset and/or mobile number.
- The application-based mobile banking can also communicate using SMS and GPRS (data) channels with the mobile banking system of the bank.

6.2.4 Challenges Faced by Banks: Despite the potential for mobile banking and the regulatory provisions enabling greater use of mobiles as a channel for financial services in general, and for financial inclusion in particular, banks are facing some challenges in taking mobile banking to the desired level. These challenges are essentially in two fronts:

1. Customer enrolment related issues.
2. Technical issues.

A. Customer Enrolment Related Issues: These are as under:

1. Mobile number registration.
2. M-PIN generation process.
3. Concerns relating to security are a factor affecting on-boarding of customers.
4. Bank staff education.
5. Customer education.

(a) Mobile Number Registration: For a customer, in order to conduct a mobile payment transaction, his/her mobile number needs to be registered with the bank. The process for mobile number registration is implemented differently across banks. Currently, the process for mobile number registration involves the following:

- Customer mandatorily needs to go to the bank branch for most of the banks to register his number and fill in the application form (paper-based). After verification, his number gets registered in the CBS and in the bank's mobile banking system.
- Some leading banks have provided the facility for

customer to register mobile number at their bank's ATMs using 2FA authentication of ATM card + ATM PIN. In both the above cases, the customer needs to physically go to the branch/ATM in order to register their mobile number, which acts as a barrier in many cases, besides delaying the entire process. Further, even where the above process of registration through ATMs is provided, it is restricted to the use of own-bank ATMs and the same is not possible at present by going to any other bank ATMs. The process for mobile number registration needs to be simpler for customer to get on-boarded.

(b) M-PIN Generation: M-PIN is the second factor of authentication that customer needs to use in order to conduct mobile banking transaction. Customer needs M-PIN from his respective bank in order to get started with mobile payments. Currently, the process for M-PIN generation is implemented differently across banks, and involves the following:

- For most banks, after the mobile number registration at branch/any bank ATM, customer receives M-PIN via SMS on their registered mobile number. In certain cases, customer receives the M-PIN through postal mail.

- Some leading banks have provided the facility for generating and changing M-PIN from the handset itself using the mobile banking application and providing the authentication parameters as required by the bank (e.g. debit card details such as debit card number, ATM PIN, expiry date). These inputs are captured and sent through registered mobile number, for the purpose of M-PIN generation.

- Some leading banks have also provided the facility to generate and change M-PIN through alternate channels such as IVR, ATM, and Internet Banking. Customer may be able to make merchant payment using just his mobile number and M-PIN/OTP on the merchant interface. The M-pin can be only interfaced on acquiring bank's interface such as USSD, Application etc. for security reasons. The merchant based interfaces can accept OTP (one-time password) for authentication.

(c) Concerns Related to Security: One of the major factors affecting customer on-boarding and usage of mobile banking services is the concern relating to security of transactions effected using the mobile phone. While mobile banking application is an end-to-end encrypted channel, the other access channels viz. SMS, USSD, IVR, are not end-to-end encrypted. However, in order to enjoy the higher level of security available in the application-based mobile banking, the customer's handset has to be GPRS-enabled.

Since SMS facility is available on all handsets, the issue of security can be addressed if the SMS can be encrypted end-to-end, thus allaying any concerns relating to lack of security in this channel.

In addition to this, another important aspect adding to the concerns on the part of customers relate to how their complaints and grievances will be addressed for transacting on this channel—whether through their bank or through their mobile service provider.

(d) Bank Staff Training: For effective and efficient implementation of providing mobile banking facilities to the customers it is imperative that the banks staff is well versed and thoroughly trained in various aspects of the mobile banking.

(e) Customer Education: Banks must continue to invest in handholding and educating customers to increase the awareness of various aspects of mobile banking. Banks collectively may invest in marketing and advertising for widespread promotion of mobile banking.

B. Technical Issues: Technical aspects which are posing a challenge relate to the following:
1. Access channels for transactions.
2. Cumbersome transaction process.
3. Co-ordination with MNOs in mobile banking eco-system.

(a) Access Channels for Transaction: Once the customer mobile number is registered and M-PIN is generated, customer may use any of the access channels provided by the bank for conducting mobile banking transactions. Currently, while most banks have provided mobile banking application and SMS facility as access channels, a few banks have also provided other access channels such as USSD, WAP, IVR, etc. Some banks also provide a combination of a few of these channels (application + SMS, application + USSD) for offering better security.

(b) Cumbersome Transaction Process: In the present scenario, with various banks offering various channels for their customers to undertake mobile banking transactions, the user experience is certainly not uniform across banks/channels. The customer is required to provide different set of inputs (authentication parameters) for each type of access channel, thus making the entire transaction process cumbersome.

(c) Co-ordination with MNOs in Mobile Banking Eco-system: In order to offer a more secure and better user experience to their customers through their mobile banking channels, banks need a greater level of coordination with the telecom service providers.

Endnotes

1. Hacking refers to the practice of breaking into a computer without authorisation, for malicious reasons, just to prove it can be done, or for other personal reasons.

2. Sniffing involves the use of a software program that is illicitly inserted somewhere on a network to capture ("sniff') user passwords as they pass through the system.

3. Spoofing refers to an attempt to gain access to a system by posing as an authorised user.

4. A denial of service attack represents an attempt to overwhelm a server with requests so that it cannot respond to legitimate traffic.

5. Identification is concerned with positively establishing the identity of the person or organisation conducting the transaction. Passwords are a common approach although evolving approaches such as biometrics may become increasingly prevalent. Authorisation is concerned with establishing the authority that an individual has to conduct a particular transaction.

6. Attacks on internal systems including those by employees are more frequent than external attacks in many organisations.

7

Digitization of Stock Exchanges

There are 21 recognised stock exchanges in India, including the Over the Counter Exchange of India (OTCEI) for small and new companies, the old established Bombay Stock Exchange (BSE) and the newer National Stock Exchange (NSE) that was set up as a model exchange to provide nation-wide services to investors. The Bombay Stock Exchange (BSE) was set up in 1875 as 'The Native Share and Stock Brokers Association'.

Equity trading is most active in the two major competing stock exchanges, viz. NSE and the BSE. Trading infrastructure in the stock exchanges is anonymous and order-driven, with all orders from market participants being matched based on strike price/time priority.

7.1 Corporatisation and Demutualisation of Stock Exchanges

The Indian capital market is significant in terms of its degree of development, its volume of trading and of the quality of its automated trading and settlement. The capital markets—though they have suffered from periodic scandals and problems in the past—look much closer in quality to those of developed markets than those in the majority of emerging markets. The range and quality of available securities is evidenced by the substantial flows of foreign institutional investors.

The competition between NSE and BSE is a unique one by international standards, where both exchanges are in the same city and have the same trading hours. All major stocks trade on both exchanges, so the exchanges compete for order flow, and not just listings. The rise of NSE has proved to be a powerful spur to reforms at the BSE. Months after NSE started operations, the BSE also launched electronic trading, and improved rules governing admission of corporate and foreign brokerage firms.

Presently, the BSE also uses an open electronic limit order book market, using satellite communications to reach locations outside Bombay.

BSE—one of the oldest exchanges in the world—accounts for the largest number of listed companies and has also started a screen-based trading system with the introduction of the Bombay On-Line Trading system. NSE—which in the recent past has accounted for the largest trading volumes—has a fully automated screen-based system that operates in the wholesale debt market segment as well as the capital market segment. BSE and NSE account for the large majority of trading volumes owing to establishment of screen-based trading and terminals in all major and many minor cities. Presently, small regional exchanges are virtually moribund.

Associated with the NSE are the National Securities Depositary Ltd. (NSDL) and the National Securities Clearing Corporation Ltd (NSCCL). The NSDL acts as the registrar for what are now predominantly dematerialized securities and the NSCCL as a clearing house.

The setting up of the NSE as an electronic trading platform set a benchmark of operating efficiency for other stock exchanges in the country. The establishment of NSDL in 1996 and Central Depository Services (India) Ltd. (CSDL) in 1999 has enabled paperless trading in the exchanges. This has also facilitated instantaneous electronic transfer of securities and eliminated the risks to the investors arising from bad deliveries in the market, delays in share transfer, fake and forged shares and loss of scrips. The electronic funds transfer (EFT) facility combined with dematerialisation of shares has created a conducive environment for reducing the settlement cycle in stock markets.

Stock exchanges all over the world have been traditionally formed as *mutual* organisations. The trading members not only provide broking services, but also own, control and manage such exchanges for their mutual benefit. In India, NSE was set up as a demutualised corporate body, where ownership, management and trading rights are in the hands of three different sets of groups from its inception. The Stock Exchange, Mumbai—one of the two premier exchanges in the country—has since been corporatised and demutualised and renamed as the Bombay Stock Exchange Ltd. (BSE).

Corporate governance has emerged as an important tool for protection of shareholders. The corporate governance framework in India has evolved over a period of time since the setting up of the Kumar Mangalam Birla Committee by SEBI. According to the Economic Intelligence Unit Survey of corporate governance across the countries (2003), India was rated the third best country to have good corporate governance code after Singapore and Hong Kong. India has a reasonably well-designed regulatory framework for the issuance and trading of securities, and disclosures by the issuers with strong focus on corporate governance standards.

To enhance the level of continuous disclosure by the listed companies, SEBI amended the listing agreement to incorporate segment reporting, related party disclosures, consolidated financial results and consolidated financial statements. The listing agreement between the stock exchanges and the companies has been strengthened from time to time to enhance corporate governance standards.

7.2 Depository System, Dematerialisation (Demat) and Rematerialisation

7.2.1 Depository System: Shares are traditionally held in physical (paper) form. This method has weaknesses like loss/theft of certificates, forged/fake certificates, cumbersome and time consuming procedure for transfer of shares etc. To eliminate these weaknesses, a new system called depository system has been established. A depository is a system which holds shares of an investor in the form of electronic accounts in the same way a bank holds money of a depositor in a savings account.

A depository holds securities in dematerialised form. It

maintains ownership records of securities in a book entry form and also effects transfer of ownership through book entry. Depository system provides the following advantages to an investor:

1. Shares cannot be lost, stolen or mutilated.
2. An investor never needs to doubt the genuineness of his shares i.e. whether they are forged or fake.
3. Share transactions like transfer, transmission etc. can be effected immediately.
4. Transaction costs are usually lower than on the physical segment.
5. There is no risk of bad delivery.
6. Bonus/rights shares allotted to an investor will be immediately credited to his account.
7. An investor receives the statement of accounts of his transactions/holdings periodically.

SEBI has introduced some degree of compulsion in trading and settlement of securities in demat form while the investors have a right to hold securities in either physical or demat form, SEBI has mandated compulsory trading and settlement of securities in select securities in dematerialised form. This was initially introduced for institutional investors and was later extended to all investors.

7.2.2 Dematerialisation (Demat): The concept of demat was introduced in Indian capital market in 1996 with the setting up of NSDL. Demat is the process by which the physical certificates of an investor are converted to an equivalent number of securities in electronic form and credited in the investor's account with his depository participant (DP).

When an investor decides to have his shares in electronic form, he should approach a depository participant (DP)—who is an agent of the depository—and open an account. He should then request for the dematerialisation of certificates by filling up a dematerialisation request form (DRF), which is available with the DP and submitting the same along with the physical certificates.

The investor has to ensure that before the certificates are handed over to the DP for demat, they are defaced by marking *surrendered for dematerialisation* on the face of the certificates. Before defacing the share certificate, the investor must ensure that it is available for dematerialisation. The investor must therefore check with his depository participant (DP) whether the ISIN (code number for the security in a depository system) has been activated and made available for dematerialisation by the depository. If yes, then the investor may deface the share certificate. Only those certificates can be dematerialised that are already registered in the investor's name and are in the list of securities admitted for dematerialization by National Securities Depository Limited (NSDL).

His DP will arrange to get them sent to and verified by the company, and on confirmation credit his account with an equivalent number of shares. This process is known as dematerialisation (demat). An investor can always reverse this process if he so desires and get his shares reconverted into paper format. This process is known as rematerialisation.

The benefits of demat are the following:

1. Elimination of bad deliveries.
2. Elimination of all risks associated with physical certification.
3. No stamp duty.
4. Immediate transfer and registration of securities.
5. Faster settlement cycle.
6. Faster disbursement of rights, bonus etc.
7. Reduction in brokerage by many brokers for trading in dematerialised securities.
8. Reduction in handling of huge volumes of paper and postal delays.
9. Periodic status report.
10. Elimination of problems relating to change of address of investor, transmission etc.
11. Elimination of problems related to selling securities on behalf of a minor.
12. Ease in portfolio monitoring.

7.2.3 Rematerialisation: If the investor wishes to get back his securities in physical form, all he has to do is to request his DP for rematerialisation of the same. Rematerialisation is the term used for converting electronic holdings back into certificates. An investor's DP will forward his request to NSDL, after verifying that he has the necessary balance. NSDL in turn will intimate the registrar who will print the certificates and dispatch the same to the investor.

7.3 Infrastructure for Government Securities Market

As part of financial sector reforms, the RBI has taken several initiatives for developing the technological infrastructure for the efficient functioning of the government securities market. These measures were accompanied by an assessment of the risk management systems under the new institutional arrangements.

7.3.1 Trading Infrastructure: An efficient government securities market requires a system of transparent pricing and allotment mechanism which reduces transaction cost and improves market efficiency. In June 1994, the National Stock Exchange (NSE) introduced a transparent fully-automated screen-based trading system known as National Exchange for Automated Trading (NEAT) in the wholesale debt market (WDM) segment for facilitating trading in various debt instruments, including government securities.

In order to facilitate easier access, wider reach and active participation in the government securities market, a facility of retail trading in stock exchanges, *viz.* National Stock Exchange (NSE), Bombay Stock Exchange (BSE) and Over the Counter Exchange of India (OTCEI) was provided from January 16, 2003. Primary (urban) co-operative banks and FIs were permitted to transact in dated Central Government securities— in dematerialised form on automated order-driven systems of stock exchanges—from March 13, 2003 and from June 1, 2003, respectively.

7.3.2 Negotiated Dealing System (NDS): The Negotiated

Dealing System (NDS) was operationalised from February 15, 2002 to provide, *inter alia*, an online electronic bidding platform for primary auctions in Central/State Government securities and OMO/LAF auctions.

The RBI introduced the NDS with the objectives of: (a) ushering in an automated electronic reporting and settlement process, (b) facilitating online electronic bidding in primary auctions and (c) providing an electronic dealing platform for trading in government securities in the secondary market. The NDS, which is available on a secure network, i.e. Indian Financial Network (INFINET) to a closed user group, facilitates straight-through settlement of secondary market transactions, thereby enhancing transparency and transactional efficiency. The NDS has greatly enhanced operational efficiency of the market by automating the flow of traded data into the settlement system. It has also facilitated dissemination of price information almost on a real time basis to market participants, enabling them to execute trading decision more effectively. The NDS has, however, gained popularity more as a reporting platform for the trade concluded bilaterally in OTC markets than as a trading platform as originally envisaged.

In order to provide the NDS members with a more efficient trading platform, the NDS-Order Matching (NDS-OM) trading module was operationalised on August 1, 2005 on the basis of the recommendations of the Working Group on Screen-based Trading in Government Securities (Chairman: R.H. Patil).

The NDS-OM is an anonymous order matching system which allows straight-through processing (STP). It is purely order-driven with all the orders matched on a strict price/time priority basis. The executed trades flow straight to the Clearing Corporation of India Ltd. (CCIL) in a ready-for-settlement stage. The CCIL is the central counterparty to each trade undertaken on the system. Participants have the option of using the NDS or the NDS-OM for their trading operations. The settlement of both types of transactions is, however, integrated.

In the first phase of operationalisation of NDS-OM, only RBI regulated entities, i.e. banks, PDs and FIs were permitted to access the system. Subsequently, insurance companies were also allowed access. Those insurance companies, which did not have a current account with the RBI, were allowed to open a special current account with it.

Consequent to the announcement made in the Union Budget for 2006-07, access to NDS-OM was further extended to all qualified mutual funds, provident funds and pension funds. While large participants in these categories can have a direct access to NDS-OM system by obtaining the direct membership, small participants are envisaged to access the system through their principal member (CSGL route). The NDS-OM system has been well received by market participants as it enhances operational and transactional efficiencies. This system has provided an efficient price discovery mechanism, reducing intra-day price volatility.

7.3.3 Clearing Corporation of India Ltd. (CCIL): CCIL was established in April 2001 to act as the clearing house and as a central counterparty for transactions in government securities. The CCIL has 172 members participating in the securities settlement segment. The establishment of CCIL has ensured guaranteed settlement of trades in government securities, thereby imparting considerable stability to the markets. Through the multilateral netting arrangement, this mechanism has reduced funding requirements from gross to net basis, thereby reducing liquidity risk and greatly mitigating counterparty credit risk. The CCIL has been equipped with the risk management system to limit the settlement risk.

Operational guidelines were issued to the CCIL in April 2003 for a limited purpose government securities lending scheme. Accordingly, the CCIL has been permitted to enter into an arrangement with any of its members for borrowing government securities for the purpose of handling securities shortage in settlement. All transactions in government securities concluded or reported on NDS as well as transactions on the NDS-OM have to be necessarily settled through the CCIL. The net obligations of members are arrived at by the CCIL for both funds and securities and then sent to the RBI for settlement under the DvP mechanism. As a step towards introducing the national settlement system (NSS) with the aim of settling centrally the clearing positions of various clearing houses, the integration of the integrated accounting system (IAS) with the real time gross settlement system (RTGS) was initiated in August, 2006. This facilitates settlement of various CCIL-operated clearings (inter-bank government securities, inter-bank foreign exchange, CBLO and National Financial Switch) through multilateral net settlement batch (MNSB) mode in the RTGS in Mumbai.

7.3.4 Settlement Cycle: The government securities market earlier followed both T+0 and T+1 settlement systems. In order to provide participants with more processing time and facilitate better funds and risk management, the settlement cycle for secondary market government securities transactions was standardised to T+1, effective May 11, 2005.

To sum up, the Indian capital market has become modern in terms of market infrastructure and trading and settlement practices. The capital market has also become a much safer place than it was before the reform process began. The secondary capital market in India has also become deep and liquid. There has also been a reduction in transaction costs and significant improvement in efficiency and transparency. However, the role of the domestic capital market in capital formation in the country, both directly and indirectly through mutual funds, continues to be less significant.

8

Digital Payment Systems

Payment system architecture in India is based on international benchmarks, and guiding principles. The Payment and Settlement System Act, 2007 provides a comprehensive legal framework for payment and settlement services in India for subjects like authorisation of payment system operators, netting and finality of payment and settlement. The payment system objectives of having a safe, sound, cost-effective and wide distribution network are being met in so far as the large value and countrywide payment and settlement systems are concerned. The grand vision is that cash dominant economy may transit to a predominantly non-cash dominant economy with non-cash transactions primarily in electronic mode, which is the international norm. The existing payment system is being constantly reviewed to suggest an action plan for orderly growth of the payment systems.

8.1 Importance of a Sound Payment and Settlement System

The payment and settlement systems are at the core of financial infrastructure in a country. A well-functioning payment and settlement system is crucial for the successful implementation of monetary policy and maintaining the financial stability. Central banks have, therefore, always maintained a keen interest in the development of payment and settlement system as part of their responsibilities for monetary and financial stability. In India, the development of a safe, secure and sound payment and settlement system has been the key policy objective. In this direction, the RBI, apart from performing the regulatory and supervisory functions, has also been making efforts to promote functionality and modernisation of the payment and settlement systems on an on-going basis.

A safe and efficient payment system is a prerequisite for smooth functioning of the financial markets. The conduct of monetary policy in an effective manner requires safe and efficient payment and settlement systems to facilitate transfer of funds and securities between the central bank and other participants in the financial system. An efficient and stable payment and settlement system is also a pre-condition for inter-bank money markets and other short-term credit markets through which monetary policy is transmitted. In addition, developments in the payment and settlement systems that affect the speed and realisation/availability of funds for further deployment can influence the overall demand for money in the economy.

By linking financial institutions together for the purpose of transferring monetary claims and settling payment obligations, payment and settlement system becomes a channel through which financial risks are transmitted across financial institutions and markets. Well-designed and efficiently managed systems, therefore, help in maintaining financial stability by reducing uncertainty of settlement. Settlement failures which spread to other payment and settlement systems through the contagion effect not only undermine the smooth functioning of the financial markets, but can also adversely affect the public confidence in money and efficacy of the instruments used to transfer money.

Payment and settlement systems, which constitute the backbone of the financial economy, aim at minimising the systemic risk. The payment system influences the speed, financial risk, reliability and the cost of domestic and international transactions. With the significant improvements in payment and settlement systems, depth and liquidity of various segments of the financial market can be improved.

Settlement systems in India have evolved over a period of time from physical settlement systems with considerable amount of risks to the current electronic systems with central counterparty with emphasis on risk mitigation. During the early 1990s, government securities market was opaque with limited information dissemination and inefficient pricing. The securities were held in physical form requiring execution of physical transfer forms for transfer of securities in any trade leading to inefficiencies in settling the trades. Settlement of securities and funds legs were independent of each other (non-DvP), leading to considerable settlement risks. Moreover, pre-settlement comparison and confirmation of trades was not systematised. Settlement cycles were not uniform with settlements happening on T+0 and T+1 basis.

8.2 Segments of Payment System

Payment systems in India comprise electronic payment systems as well as paper-based systems. Another classification pertains to large value payment systems and retail payment systems.

The large value payment infrastructure comprises RTGS, high value clearing, and CCIL. Based on the criteria outlined by CPSS, the RTGS system and the high value clearing system have been identified as SIPS. The funds leg of the CCIL-operated clearing systems covering government securities, foreign exchange and money market settle in the RTGS system.

The retail payment systems include MICR/non-MICR cheque clearing, national electronic funds transfer (NEFT) system, electronic clearing service (ECS), cheque truncation system (CTS) and payment channels like cards, internet and mobile phone-based products.

8.3 Large Value Payment Systems

8.3.1 Real Time Gross Settlement (RTGS) System: The Indian RTGS system was operationalised in March 2004. The system started operations with four banks and settled only inter-bank transactions. Subsequently, the system was opened for settlement of customer transactions. It was operationalised for settlement of multilateral net settlement batch (MNSB) files from September 2006.

RTGS system is owned and operated by the Reserve Bank of India (RBI). The system works on a mainframe computer. Members are provided with a participant interface (PI), using which the participants connect to the system at the RBI through the INFINET. The message flow architecture in the RTGS system uses the Y topology. The members communicate through their PI to the inter-bank funds transfer processor (IFTP) which validates all communication and also does the *strip and store* function.

Upon successful completion of a transaction and receipt of confirmation from the RTGS, the IFTP forwards the complete credit information to the beneficiary member's PI. All communication between the PI and IFTP and IFTP to RTGS uses digital signatures (public key infrastructure) to ensure security.

The membership of RTGS is open to all scheduled commercial banks (SCBs), primary dealers (PDs) and others, as may be decided by the RBI. The SCBs are provided with Type A membership, primary dealers Type B and clearing houses Type D membership.

Except Type A members, customer-based transactions cannot be submitted by other members. Type D members are permitted to submit only net settlement batches for settlement under the RTGS system. Other banks and financial institutions can participate as customers of the direct members.

RTGS operations are governed by the RTGS Membership Regulations, 2004 and RTGS (Membership) Business Operating Guidelines, 2004. The members of the system agree to abide by these regulations and guidelines and any subsequent amendments to these documents.

The settlement of RTGS transactions takes place in the books of the RBI. For this purpose, members have to open a 'RTGS Settlement Account' with the RBI at Mumbai. This account is to be funded at the beginning of each RTGS processing day from the member's current account with the RBI, and at the end of the day, the balance in the settlement account is transferred back to the current account of the member.

Members are provided with collateralized intra-day liquidity (IDL) facility to tide over their IDL mis-matches. This facility is provided to Type A and Type B members only. The IDL facility utilised by the members has to necessarily be reversed by them at the end of RTGS day. Failure to do so attracts penal action. In addition to IDL, the system provides many features for effective liquidity management by the members. These include message release method, queuing management and queue visibility. The Indian RTGS has adopted the FIFO rule for queuing. The system has a centralised queuing arrangement with priorities assigned by the system participant. The participant/system operator can change the priority of messages/revoke the messages in the queue. The system operator would alter the queue only in extreme situations. At the end of the day, all pending unsettled messages are cancelled by the system. The system has a multilateral offsetting algorithm to resolve any gridlock situations that may arise. This process can be configured to be invoked manually or automatically by the system. Since it is mainly a large-value funds transfer system, a floor of ₹ 2 lakh has been prescribed for minimum value of transactions that can be settled through RTGS.

There has been a substantial increase in the volume of transactions settled through RTGS. The inter-bank clearing at all the RBI centres have been migrated to the RTGS system. Further, multilateral net settlements from CCIL, viz. rupee leg of US dollar-Indian rupee settlement, funds leg of government securities settlement and funds leg of CBLO, and the retail net settlement systems operated by National Clearing Cell, Mumbai (MICR cheque clearing, high value clearing, NEFT and ECS) are settled in RTGS as multilateral net settlement batch (MNSB) files. The liquidity management operations of the RBI are also settled through the RTGS system.

8.4 Retail Payment Systems
The retail payment systems in India consist of the paper-

based clearing systems, electronic clearing systems and those systems relating to payment cards (credit and debit).

8.4.1 Paper-based Systems (Cheques): Cheques as payment instruments are the most popular mode of non-cash payment in India. The clearing and settlement of cheques drawn on different banks require the coming together of the banks in that area for transfer of instruments and the final settlement of funds. This process was facilitated by the clearing houses at these centres. As on May 31, 2014 there were 1,396 operational clearing houses. Of these, at 66 centres, the clearing and settlement processes were automated by the introduction of MICR technology-based sorter machines. 80 percent of the total cheque clearing volume and value was accounted for by these centres. The clearing and settlement cycle is completed in two days—on day 1, the cheques are presented at the clearing house and on day 2, the funds settlement and return clearing are accounted for.

Paper-based systems still constitute the major part of retail payment systems in India. Steps taken by the Reserve Bank to improve the availability of this facility resulted in an increase in the number of clearing houses from 860 in 2001 to 1,396 as on May 31, 2014. Further, in order to increase the spread of computerised clearing houses, magnetic media-based clearing system (MMBCS) technology is also being implemented in cities and towns where the process is carried out manually at present.

The introduction of cheque truncation system (CTS) was yet another step for increasing the efficiency of retail payment system. Truncation is the process of stopping the flow of the physical cheque issued by a drawer at some point with the presenting bank enroute to the drawee bank branch. In its place, an electronic image of the cheque is transmitted to the drawee branch by the clearing house, along with relevant information like data on the MICR band, date of presentation, presenting bank, etc.

The Reserve Bank implemented the CTS in the National

Capital Region (NCR), New Delhi, Chennai and Mumbai with effect from February 1, 2008, September 24, 2011 and April 27, 2013 respectively. After migration of the entire cheque volume from MICR system to CTS, the traditional MICR-based cheque processing has been discontinued in the country. Based on the advantages realised by the stakeholders and the experienced gained from the roll-out in these centres, it was decided to operationalise CTS across the country. The new approach envisioned as part of the national roll-out is the grid-based approach. Under this approach, the entire cheque volume in the country which was earlier cleared through 66 MICR cheque processing locations is consolidated into the three grids in New Delhi, Chennai and Mumbai. Each grid provides processing and clearing services to all the banks under its respective jurisdiction.

Under grid-based cheque truncation system clearing, all cheques drawn on bank branches falling within in the grid jurisdiction are treated and cleared as local cheques.

8.4.2 Electronic Retail Payment Instruments: The retail electronic payment systems in India are national electronic funds transfer system and the electronic clearing service.

A. National Electronic Funds Transfer (NEFT): Electronic Funds Transfer (EFT) system was introduced in the mid-1990s. EFT facilitates transfer of funds from one bank account to another. The EFT system is currently only permitted to be used for government transactions and RBI-initiated payments. This system is now progressively being replaced with the National Electronic Funds Transfer (NEFT). NEFT is an electronic message-based payment system, and was introduced by the Reserve Bank of India in November 2005 to replace the EFT system which was public key infrastructure (PKI)-enabled and the settlements were effected on a decentralized mode.

NEFT is more secure, nation-wide retail electronic payment system to facilitate funds transfer by the bank customers, between the networked bank branches in the country. This has facilitated the availability of electronic payment modes at more centres.

There are 12 daily settlements during weekdays.

The banks are to credit the accounts of the customers for the first four settlements on the same day and for the fifth and sixth settlements, the customers' accounts are to be credited not later than T+1 (next working day).

As on January 7, 2017, NEFT was available at 1,34,363 branches all over the country with 178 participating banks.

In order to popularise the e-payments in the country, the RBI, on its part, waived the service charges to be levied on the member banks, till March 31, 2009, in respect of the real time gross settlement (RTGS) and NEFT transactions. The RBI also provides, free of charge, intra-day liquidity to the banks for the RTGS transactions.

The service charges to be levied by banks from their customers for RTGS and NEFT have, however, been deregulated and left to the discretion of the individual banks. While some of the banks have rationalised their service charges and a few have made it even cost-free to the customers, there are also certain banks that have fixed unreasonably high service charges for providing these services to their customers—even though the RBI provides these services to the banks free of charge.

B. Electronic Clearing Services (ECS): ECS is a retail payment system which facilitates bulk payments that can be classified as one-to-many and receipts that are many-to-one. The two components of this system are ECS (Credit) and ECS (Debit). This facility is now available at 91 major centres.

- **ECS (Credit):** It facilitates the bulk payments whereby the account of the institution remitting the payment is debited and the payments remitted to beneficiaries' accounts. This facility is mostly used for making multiple payments, like payment of dividend to investors, payment of salaries of employees by institutions etc. For this purpose, the company or entity making the payment has to have the bank account details of the individual beneficiaries.

- **ECS (Debit):** It facilitates the collection of payments by utility companies. In this system the account of the customers of the utility company in different banks are debited and the amounts are transferred to the account of the utility company. The company providing this facility has to receive the mandate to collect funds from its customer. On receipt of the mandate, the company advises the consumer's bank to debit the payment due from the account on the due dates.

Settlement in this system currently takes place on T+0 basis and the cycle gets completed on T+1 basis. The clearing and settlement transactions through ECS occur at the respective centres. A centralised facility is available at the RBI, Mumbai to receive the ECS (Credit) files meant for credit at the other 14 RBI centres.

8.4.3 Deficiencies in Retail Payment Systems: The deficiencies in retail payments mainly pertain to the inefficient outstation cheque collection process. In this regard, it is difficult to prescribe a standard time-frame for collection in view of large disparities at various centres, in terms of their location, availability of infrastructure, communication facilities, etc. In respect of metropolitan cities, State capitals and A class cities, most banks have a policy of collecting instruments within a period of 7 to 10 days. In respect of other cities including States in the North-eastern region, most banks have declared in their policies that the instruments will be collected within a maximum period of 14 days.

The usage of ECS has seen rapid increase. The main deficiency in ECS system has been the decentralised model of transaction processing in the system. While a centralised ECS has been provided, this is available only at the RBI centres. To address this deficiency, a National Electronic Clearing Platform was implemented in September 2008.

The benefits of electronic payment infrastructure are not yet trickling down to the lower end of the customer segment which still largely uses services like money order and informal channels for transferring money of small value which has much higher cost and time lag for transferring money. There is a need to develop solutions using newer technologies which would allow all segments of the society to gain access to the benefits offered by these facilities.

In order to popularise the e-payments in the country, the RBI, on its part, waived the service charges levied on the member banks till March 31, 2009, in respect of the RTGS and NEFT transactions. The RBI also provides, free of charge, intra-day liquidity to the banks for the RTGS transactions. The service charges to be levied by banks from their customers for RTGS and NEFT have, however, been deregulated and left to discretion of the individual bank. While some of the banks have rationalised their service charges and a few have made it even cost-free to the customers, there are also certain banks that have fixed multiples slabs or unreasonably high service charges, at times linked to the amount of the transaction, for providing these services to their customers, even though the RBI provides these services to the banks free of charge.

8.4.4 Vision Document for Payment Systems, 2012-15: The main focus of the Vision Document for Payments Systems, 2012-15 is to provide a thrust to modern electronic payments that are safe, simple and low-cost for use by all. The document aims at increasing the share of electronic payment transactions and taking measures towards moving to a less cash society and customer convenience.

The focus of cheque clearing operations in the coming years would be consolidation, rationalisation, centralisation, through the implementation of grid-based CTS solution (which is Information Technology Act compliant) across the country by NPCI. The grid-based CTS will usher in a standardised cheque clearing scenario across the country. The issuance of CTS 2010 compliant cheques will facilitate this process. Introduction of user/customer friendly features and increasing the number of settlement cycles in NEFT would be further examined.

8.5 National Payments Corporation of India (NPCI)

NPCI is an umbrella organization for all retail payments system in India. It was set up with the guidance and support of the Reserve Bank of India (RBI) and Indian Banks' Association (IBA).

The RBI, after setting up the Board for Regulation and Supervision of Payment and Settlement Systems (BPSS) in 2005, released a vision document incorporating a proposal to set up an umbrella institution for all the Retail Payment Systems in the country. The core objective was to consolidate and integrate the multiple systems with varying service levels into nation-wide uniform and standard business process for all retail payment systems. The other objective was to facilitate an affordable payment mechanism to benefit the common man across the country and help financial inclusion.

IBA's untiring efforts during the last few years helped to turn this vision into a reality. NPCI was incorporated in December 2008 and the Certificate of Commencement of Business was issued in April 2009. It was incorporated as a Section 25 company under Companies Act, 1956 (now Section 8 of Companies Act 2013) and is aimed to operate for the benefit of all the member banks and their customers. The authorized capital is pegged at ₹ 300 crore and paid-up capital is ₹ 100 crore. The aim is to create infrastructure of large dimension and operate on high volumes resulting in payment services at a fraction of the present cost structure.

NPCI has ten promoter banks, namely State Bank of India, Punjab National Bank, Canara Bank, Bank of Baroda, Union Bank of India, Bank of India, ICICI Bank, HDFC Bank, Citibank and HSBC.

From a single service of switching of inter-bank ATM transactions, the range of services has grown to cheque clearing, immediate payments service (24x7x365), automated clearing house, electronic benefit transfer and a domestic card payment network named RuPay to provide an alternative to international card schemes. As in January 2016, over 247 million Indians owned RuPay cards. During the week following the demonetization, RuPay card usage increased by 118.6 percent.

BPSS at its meeting held on September 24, 2009 had given

an in-principle approval to issue authorization to NPCI for operating various retail payment systems in the country and granted Certificate of Authorization for operation of National Financial Switch (NFS) ATM Network with effect from October 15, 2009. NPCI had deputed its officials to IDRBT Hyderabad and had taken over NFS operations on December 14, 2009. Membership regulations and rules had been framed for enrolling all banks in the country as members. This was done so that when the nation-wide payment systems are launched, all would get included on a standardized platform.

8.6 Committee to Review the Framework Related to Digital Payments

Ministry of Finance, Government of India had constituted this Committee on Digital Payments to review the payment systems in the country and to recommend appropriate measures for encouraging digital payments. The Committee (Chairman: Ratan P. Watal) was constituted on August 23, 2016 with the following terms of reference:

1. To study and recommend need for charges, if any, in the regulatory mechanism and any legislation, relevant for the purpose of promotion of payments by digital modes.
2. To study and recommend ways for leveraging Unique Identification Number or any other proof of identity for authentication of card/digital transactions and setting up of a Centralised KYC Registry.
3. To study introduction of single window system of Payment Gateway to accept all types of cards/digital payments of Government receipts.
4. To study feasibility and framing rules for creating a payments history of all digital payments and create necessary linkages between payments transaction history and credit information.
5. To study and recommend various measures to incentivize transactions through cards and digital means.
6. To study global best practices in payments including initiatives taken by various Governments/Government Agencies.

7. To identify market failure(s), if any, along with suitable interventions that may be implemented to promote payment by card/digital means.

8. To identify regulatory bottlenecks, if any, and suggest changes to promote payment by card/digital means.

9. To study and make recommendations on any other matter related to promotion of payments through cards and digital means.

The Committee submitted an Interim Report to the Ministry of Finance on November 21, 2016. Towards finalization of the report, the Committee engaged extensively with all stakeholders and technology groups including Reserve Bank of India (RBI), State Governments, Comptroller and Auditor General of India, payment companies, technology companies and the academia. The Committee submitted its Final Report to the Finance Minister on December 9, 2016.

8.6.1 Recommendations: The Committee, inter alia, recommended a medium-term strategy for accelerating growth of digital payments in India with a regulatory regime which is conducive to bridging the *digital divide* by promoting competition, open access and inter-operability in payments. The Committee recommended inclusion of financially and socially excluded groups and assimilation of emerging technologies in the market, while safeguarding security of digital transactions and providing level playing to all stakeholders and new players who will enter this new transaction space. It suggested inter-operability of the payments system between banks and non-banks, upgradation of the digital payment infrastructure and institutions and a framework to reward innovations and for leading efforts in enabling digital payments. This Committee was seized of the developments following the decision of the Government to cancel legal tender character of currency of high denominations. The Committee calibrated its recommendations accordingly and provided a suitable framework for smooth and speedy transition towards a digital payments economy.

8.7 Benefits of Electronic Payments
8.7.1 Common Man:
- Reduced cash and hence more safety.
- Faster payment.
- Reduced number of visits to bank.
- Interest earning on money in the bank.

8.7.2 Vendors:
- Transactions settled quickly.
- Getting rid of coins and change.
- Larger transactions made easy.
- Improved accounting and book keeping.
- No need to keep large amounts of cash.

8.8 Credit/Debit Cards

In recent years advancements in banking technology, progress in mobile banking and innovative technologies to facilitate digital payments have enabled large number of small denomination transactions to be handled smoothly in electronic mode. The Government of India has taken policy decisions to encourage cashless/electronic transactions. In its endeavour on moving towards electronic payments, the Central Government has announced a number of incentives.

A credit card is a payment card issued to users (cardholders) to enable the cardholder to pay a merchant for goods and services, based on the cardholder's promise to the card issuer to pay them for the amounts so paid plus other agreed charges. The card issuer (usually a bank) creates a revolving account and grants a line of credit to the cardholder, from which the cardholder can borrow money for payment to a merchant or as a cash advance.

A debit card is a plastic payment card that can be used instead of cash when making purchases. It is similar to a credit card, but unlike a credit card, the money comes directly from the user's bank account when performing a transaction.

There has been phenomenal increase in the number of credit cards issued by the banks in India during the last few years. The number of outstanding credit cards at end-October

2016 stood at 2.73 crore.

While the increasing usage of the credit cards is a welcome development in as much as it reduces reliance on currency for settlement of transactions, it also entails certain additional elements of operational risk and can be a potential source of customer complaints.

In order to ensure orderly growth of the card segment of consumer credit and protect the interests of banks/non-banking financial companies (NBFCs) and their customers, the RBI constituted a Working Group on Regulatory Mechanism for Cards (Chairman: R. Gandhi).

Based of the recommendations of the Working Group, draft guidelines on credit cards were framed by the RBI in June 2005 for all commercial banks/NBFCs with regard to their credit card operations.

The draft guidelines delineated the broad parameters that banks/NBFCs should, at the minimum, take into account with regard to the following:

1. Issue of cards with respect to clear mentioning of most important terms and conditions (MITCs).
2. Interest rates and other charges on customers.
3. Corrective mechanism on account of wrongful billing.
4. Use of direct sale agents and other agents for outsourcing various credit card operations.
5. Protection of customer rights especially in respect of right to privacy, customer confidentiality and fair practices in debt collection.
6. Redressal avenues of customer grievances.
7. Internal control and monitoring systems of the banks/NBFCs for such card operations.

The draft guidelines further stipulated that each bank/NBFC must have a well-documented policy and a *fair practices code* for credit card operations. The *fair practices code* for credit card operations released by the IBA in March 2005 could also be used by banks/NBFCs. The bank/NBFCs code should, at the minimum, however, incorporate the relevant guidelines contained in the draft guidelines released by the RBI.

8.9 ATM Networks

The main advantage of an ATM network is that it obviates the need for having bank-specific multiple ATM installations in the same geographical area, thereby reducing the entailed costs for the banks but without compromising on the reach of the banks to their customers.

Over the years, the relative growth in off-site ATMs has been much more than that of on-site ATMs. As a result, by end October 2016, off-site ATMs accounted for approximately 47.63 percent (97,731) of the total ATMs in the country. With the policy initiative to enable non-bank entities to set up and operate ATMs—White Label ATMs (WLAs)—the proportion of off-site ATMs is likely to grow further.

The National Financial Switch (NFS) network started its operations on August 27, 2004. NFS is one of the several shared ATM networks which inter-connect the ATM switches of the banks together and thus enable inter-operability of the ATM cards issued by any bank across the entire network. The Board for Regulation and Supervision of Payment and Settlement systems (BPSS) approved in-principle to issue authorisation to National Payments Corporation of India (NPCI) for operating various retail payment systems in the country. Reserve Bank of India also issued authorisation to NPCI to take over the operations of National Financial Switch (NFS) from the Institute of Development and Research in Banking Technology (IDRBT) on October 15, 2009. NPCI took over NFS operations from December 14, 2009. Use of the ATMs connected through any of the ATM networks in the country became cost free for the customers from April 1, 2009.

As at end-October 2016, the number of ATMs in the country stood at 2,05,151.

8.10 Digital Wallet

Digital wallet refers to an electronic device that allows an individual to make electronic transactions. This can include purchasing items online with a computer or using a smartphone to purchase something at a store. An individual's bank account can also be linked to the digital wallet. He may also have his driver's license, health card, loyalty card(s) and other ID documents stored on the phone. The credentials can be passed to a merchant's terminal wirelessly via near field communication (NFC). Increasingly, digital wallets are being made not just for basic financial transactions but to also authenticate the holder's credentials. For example, a digital wallet could potentially verify the age of the buyer to the store while purchasing alcohol. The system has already gained popularity in Japan, where digital wallets are known as "wallet mobiles".

A digital wallet has both a software and information component. The software provides security and encryption for the personal information and for the actual transaction. Typically, digital wallets are stored on the client side and are easily self-maintained and fully compatible with most e-commerce websites. A server-side digital wallet, also known as a thin wallet, is one that an organization creates for and about you and maintains on its servers. Server-side digital wallets are gaining popularity among major retailers due to the security, efficiency, and added utility it provides to the end-user, which increases their satisfaction of their overall purchase. The information component is basically a database of user-input information. This information consists of your shipping address, billing address, payment methods (including credit card numbers, expiry dates, and security numbers), and other information.

Digital wallet systems enable the widespread use of digital wallet transactions among various retail vendors in the form of mobile payments systems and digital wallet applications.

A client-side digital wallet requires minimal set-up and is relatively easy to use. Once the software is installed, the user begins by entering all the pertinent information. The digital wallet is now set up. At the purchase or check-out page of an e-commerce site, the digital wallet software has the ability to automatically enter the user information in the online form. By default, most digital wallets prompt when the software recognizes a form in which it can fill out; if one chooses to fill out the form automatically, the user will be prompted for a password. This keeps unauthorized users away from viewing personal information stored on a particular computer.

8.10.1 Application of Digital Wallets: Consumers are not required to fill out order forms on each site when they purchase an item because the information has already been stored and is automatically updated and entered into the order fields across merchant sites when using a digital wallet. Consumers also benefit when using digital wallets because their information is encrypted or protected by a private software code; merchants benefit by receiving protection against fraud.

Digital wallets are available to consumers free of charge, and they are fairly easy to obtain. For example, when a consumer makes a purchase at a merchant site that is set up to handle server-side digital wallets, he types his name and payment and shipping information into the merchant's own form. At the end of the purchase, the consumer is asked to sign up for a wallet of his choice by entering a user name and password for future purchases. Users can also acquire wallets at a wallet vendor's site.

Although a wallet is free for consumers, vendors charge merchants for wallets. Some wallet vendors make arrangements for merchants to pay them a percentage of every successful purchase directed through their wallets. In other cases, digital wallet vendors process the transactions between cardholders and participating merchants and charge merchants a flat fee.

8.10.2 Advantages for E-commerce Sites: Many online shoppers abandon their order due to frustration in filling in forms. The digital wallet combats this problem by giving users the option to transfer their information securely and accurately.

This simplified approach to completing transactions results in better usability and ultimately more utility for the customer.

Digital wallets can also increase the security of the transaction since the wallet typically does not pass payment card details to the website (a unique transaction identifier or token is shared instead). Increasingly this approach is a feature of online payment gateways, especially if the payment gateway offers a *hosted payment page* integration approach.

8.11 Aadhaar-enabled Payment System (AEPS)

AEPS is a bank led model which allows online interoperable financial inclusion transaction at PoS (Micro-ATM) through the Business Correspondent of any bank using the Aadhaar authentication.

The four Aadhaar enabled basic types of banking transactions are as follows:

1. Balance enquiry.
2. Cash withdrawal.
3. Cash deposit.
4. Aadhaar-to-Aadhaar funds transfer. ,

The only inputs required for a customer to do a transaction under this method are the following:

1. IIN (Identifying the bank to which the customer is associated).
2. Aadhaar number.
3. Fingerprints captured during the enrolment

8.11.1 Objectives: These are as under:

1. To empower a bank customer to use Aadhaar as his identity to access his respective Aadhaar enabled bank account and perform basic banking transactions like balance enquiry, cash deposit, cash withdrawal, remittances that are intra-bank or inter-bank in nature, through a Business Correspondent.
2. To sub-serve the goal of Government of India and Reserve Bank of India (RBI) in furthering Financial Inclusion.
3. To sub-serve the goal of RBI in electronification of retail payments.

4. To enable banks to route the Aadhaar initiated inter-bank transactions through a central switching and clearing agency.
5. To facilitate disbursements of Government entitlements like NREGA, Social Security Pension, Handicapped Old Age Pension etc. of any Central or State Government bodies, using Aadhaar and authentication thereof as supported by UIDAI.
6. To facilitate inter-operability across banks in a safe and secured manner.
7. To build the foundation for a full range of Aadhaar-enabled banking services.

AEPS is a new payment service offered by the National Payments Corporation of India to banks, financial institutions using Aadhaar. This is known as Aadhaar-enabled Payment System and may also be referred to as AEPS.

Aadhaar is a unique identification number issued by the Unique Identification Authority of India (UIDAI) to any resident of India.

Any resident of India holding an Aadhaar number and having a bank account may be a part of the Aadhaar-enabled Payment System. Also, the customer needs to have a bank account for availing AEPS.

Customer should have an Aadhaar (Unique ID as issued by UIDAI) number linked with any bank account (bank should be a part of AEPS network) where customer has an account. The registration process shall be as per the procedures laid down by the bank providing AEPS service.

A customer may visit a Business Correspondent (BC) Customer Access Point. The BC [1] using the point of sale (Micro-ATM) device will be able to process transactions like cash withdrawal, cash deposit, balance enquiry and fund transfer by selecting the transaction of their choice. The customer needs to provide his Aadhaar Number and his bank name or bank IIN number. [2]

A Point of Sale-PoS (Micro-ATM) device is used to facilitate customers to make cash deposit, cash withdrawal, fund transfer and balance enquiry. The PoS device may be a Micro-ATM.

8.12 Unified Payment Interface (UPI) of India

UPI is a payment system which facilitates the fund transfer between two bank accounts. This payment system works on the mobile platform. Sending money through the UPI app is as easy as sending a message. The customer is not required to give bank account details for the funds transfer through the UPI payment system.

8.12.1 Benefits of UPI: What is UPI App: These are as under:

1. UPI transfers the fund immediately. No restriction of holiday or working hours. The bank strike will also not affect the UPI payments.
2. Customer does not require the bank account number and IFSC code of the recipient.
3. Customer can transact from many bank account through a single UPI app.
4. Customer is not required to wait up to 24 hours to send money to a new payee. Anyone would get money immediately.
5. Customer can send bills and get money once the client approves it.
6. Customer can use the cash on delivery without paying cash to the delivery boy. Just approve the bill and the delivery boy would get confirmation.

Although IMPS method transfers fund immediately (24x7) yet UPI has some advantages.

To send the money through the UPI, the user does not need to know about the bank of the recipient. It is necessary in the case of IMPS. To use the IMPS, the customer needs the bank account number and IFSC code of the recipient.

Only through the UPI, the customer can ask for the payments through the banking channel. In fact, one touch would complete the payment. One cannot pay for online shopping through the IMPS. But UPI gives the easiest way of online payment.

8.12.2 Virtual Payment Address (VPA): The UPI payment system does not use the bank account details of the recipient. But, there should be an accurate identification of the money recipient. Ultimately, all this convenience is fruitful if the money goes in right hands.

Therefore, every user of the UPI apps must have a unique ID. This unique ID is called as the virtual payment address (VPA). In fact, the App provider bank would allot the VPA to each user. The user can choose the VPA similar to the mail address. One can give this VPA to anyone to receive the money. The app would itself keep storing the VPAs of the persons to whom you have transferred the money. It is like saving contacts in email.

UPI payment system works only through the mobile application. Thus, you need a smartphone and internet data pack.

There are several UPI apps. You can choose any of them. Each bank can launch its UPI-based app. Banks can also incorporate UPI features into their existing mobile application. In fact, most of the banks have incorporated UPI in their existing mobile application.

UPI has made the fund transfer very easy. But it is not a mobile wallet. Unlike the mobile wallet, you are not required to credit money into the UPI app.

Rather, the every fund transfers take place through your bank account. UPI app just acts as the link between you and your account. In other words, it has made the bank account transaction much easy and cheap.

Therefore, to establish the link between you and your account, you have to connect UPI app to your bank account. This is a one-time process. It is done when you download a new UPI app.

While connecting to the bank account, you have to authenticate it through the card details and OTP. Once your UPI app gets connected to a bank account, you can easily transfer funds to any person.

The UPI payment system is revolutionary. It makes the non-cash payment a very easy affair. Moreover, the NPCI is coming with new features of UPI. Soon the UPI 2.0 would be launched which has more flexibility, easy and wide reach. You should adopt this method of payment because it also reduces the black economy.

8.13 Unstructured Supplementary Service Data (USSD): *99# Banking

Mobile banking has brought the bank account in your hand. Today, you can check bank-balance, get a mini statement and transfer fund through the mobile banking. But, what if you do not have a smart phone or you do not have the internet? The answer to this problem is the USSD based mobile banking. Just dial *99# and see the magic. You can do all those things which are available to a person with smartphone and 3G data. Almost every bank supports *99# USSD mobile banking service.

You get the mobile balance by dialling a certain code. Similarly, the recharge vendor uses certain codes to access mobile services. These are, in fact, USSD codes. The code which directly communicates with the server of telecom company is called as the USSD. This code starts with * (asterisk) and ends with # (hash).

As USSD code connects to the telecom operator's server, it also connects to bank's server. Hence, it gives you access to your bank account and performs some transaction. The entry to your bank account is given on the basis of registered mobile number. Thus, you must use registered mobile number to dial the USSD code.

The connection to the server of your bank goes through the servers of telecom companies. The NPCI handles all the technicality of this USSD service.

A special number *99# is fixed to access the banking services. This number works across the banks. This system of banking transaction is termed as the NUUP.

National Unified USSD Platform (NUUP) is an innovative service developed by NPCI and launched by the Indian government in 2014. The service allows the banks and telecom service providers to work together seamlessly. The services of NUUP are based on the USSD method.

USSD is a technology normally used in the field of telecommunication. It is available on all GSM enabled handsets. You do not need an internet connection to use the services of this method. It uses voice connectivity only.

NUUP uses USSD to perform various financial, non-financial and value added services. You can not only check your balance and see mini statement but also send money. There are some more options such as show MMID, generate OTP and change M-PIN.

8.13.1 How to Use USSD Code for Banking: First of all, you need to register your mobile number to your bank account. Visit your branch to get your mobile number registered. If your mobile number is already registered then you can directly dial the *99#. Follow these steps for USSD banking:

Step 1: Dial *99# with your registered number and wait for 3-5 seconds.

Step 2: Enter the three letter abbreviation of your bank name or first four-letter of bank IFSC or first two digits of bank's numeric code and hit send or call button.

Step 3: You will see some options for the services. It can be different for different banks. These options are as under:

1. Account balance.
2. Mini statement.
3. Send money using MMID.
4. Send money using IFSC.
5. Send money using Aadhaar number.
6. Show MMID.
7. Change M-PIN.
8. Generate OTP.

From here, the process will be different for every service.

8.14 RuPay

RuPay is an Indian domestic card scheme conceived and launched by the National Payments Corporation of India (NPCI). It was created to fulfil the Reserve Bank of India's desire to have a domestic, open loop, and multilateral system of payments in India. In India, 90 percent of credit card transactions and almost all debit card transactions are domestic. However, the cost of transactions was high due to' monopoly of foreign gateways like Visa and MasterCard. In recent years, the usage of credit and debit cards (called plastic money) has increased manifold. It was thought that if this process of transactions is made India-centric, cost can come down drastically. RuPay facilitates electronic payment at all Indian banks and financial institutions, and competes with MasterCard and Visa in India. NPCI maintains ties with Discover Financial to enable the card scheme to gain international acceptance.

RuPay is a portmanteau of the words *ru*pee and *pay*ment. The colors used in the logo are an allusion to the tricolor national flag.

RuPay card was launched on March 26, 2012. NPCI entered into a strategic partnership with Discover Financial Services (DFS) for RuPay Card, enabling the acceptance of RuPay Global Cards on Discover's global payment network outside of India.

RuPay cards are accepted at all ATMs across India under National Financial Switch, and under the NPCI's agreement with DFS, RuPay cards are accepted on the international Discover network. According to the data published by National Payments Corporation of India, there are around 145,270 ATMs and more than 875,000 point of sale (PoS) terminals in India under the RuPay platform. In addition to the ATMs and PoS terminals, RuPay cards are accepted online on 10,000 e-commerce websites.

RuPay cards are accepted at all PoS terminals in India. To enable this, RuPay has certified 29 major banks in India to accept the RuPay card at their respective PoS terminals located at different merchant locations.

To sum up, several steps have been taken by the RBI in

recent years to improve customer service of commercial banks. In the context of the rapidly evolving financial landscape, RBI has also been suitably reorienting its regulatory and supervisory framework to meet the needs of the common man. It has also been the endeavour of RBI to improve credit delivery and customer service by banks. RBI has simultaneously focussed on financial inclusion and extension of banking services to the unbanked areas of the economy. RBI has taken a host of measures in recent years aimed at providing customer service at reasonable cost. These measures include enhancing customer protection and disclosures, code of ethics and grievance redressal, among others. RBI's broad approach to financial inclusion aims at *connecting people* with the banking system and not just credit dispensation; giving people access to the payments system; and portraying financial inclusion as a viable business model and opportunity. RBI has been initiating measures to improve the outreach of banks and their services, and promote financial inclusion in less developed states and union territories.

As is well-known, the financial sector has witnessed a quantum jump in the availability of technological solutions for delivery of financial services, and the RBI too has launched several payment system products for improving the efficiency of the payment system.

Endnotes

1. Business Correspondent (BC) is an approved bank agent providing basic banking service using a MicroATM (terminal) to any bank customer wishing to avail their bank BC service.
2. IIN identifies the bank with which a customer has mapped his Aadhaar number. IIN is a six digit number. In most banks BC customer service points, this number would be represented on the terminal by the banks logo or name.

9

Electronic Money (E-money) and Electronic Commerce (E-commerce)

In recent years, there has been a gradual switchover from the use of paper-based payments media to those based on electronics. While the basic characteristics of these new instruments are by and large similar to those of paper-based instruments, the former present a different set of challenges to policy makers. E-money is one such new product which has appeared on Indian horizon recently.

9.1 Electronic Money (E-money)

9.1.1 Meaning and Kinds of E-money: E-money may be broadly defined as an electronic store of monetary value on a technical device used for making payments to undertakings other than the issuer without necessarily involving bank accounts in the transaction, but acting as a prepaid bearer instrument. E-money can be classified into the following two broad categories:

1. Pre-paid stored value card (also called electronic purse).
2. Pre-paid software-based product that uses computer networks such as internet (also referred to as digital cash or network money).

The stored value card scheme typically uses a microprocessor chip embedded in a plastic card while software based scheme typically uses specialised software installed in a personal computer. The stored value card could be of three types:

1. Single-purpose card.
2. Closed-system or limited-purpose card.
3. General-purpose or multi-purpose card.

The single-purpose card generally with a magnetic chip

recording the amount of fund therein is designed to facilitate only one type of transaction, e.g. telephone calls, public transportation, laundry, parking facilities etc. In this case the distinguishing point is that the issuer and the service provider (acceptor) are identical for the cards. These cards are expected to substitute coins and currency notes.

Closed-system or limited-purpose card is generally used in a small number of well-identified points of sale within a well-identified location such as corporate/university campus.

Multi-purpose card can perform a variety of functions with several vendors, viz. credit card, debit card, stored value card, identification card, repository of personal medical information etc. The importance of these cards is especially underscored with respect to regulatory oversight, restrictions on issuers and their implications for monetary policy. These cards may reduce demand for current accounts in the bank for likely reduction in transaction costs, and prudent portfolio management.

It is important to distinguish here the so-called *access* products, e.g. credit card and debit card from e-money. The former typically require a telephone or a personal computer with appropriate software to access the customer account before transferring the value while under e-money, the amount of value is already embedded and it may be increased or reduced without necessarily involving a personal bank account. In a sense, e-money can be construed as an electronic form of traveller's cheques (TCs). In both cases, the user pays for the instrument upfront.

9.1.2 Benefits of E-money: Use and spread of e-money depends upon the incentives of issuers, merchants and consumers. For issuers, the principal motivation arises from revenues to be earned from investment of outstanding balances (i.e. float income), savings of costs from reduced handling of cash and incentive of offering fee-based service to consumers and merchants besides the larger security emanating from audit trail of transactions and improved management information system.

For merchants, the trade-off would be between reduction in cost of handling physical cash vis-à-vis cost of putting in place necessary infrastructure.

For consumers, the use of e-money would depend upon the perceived security and privacy of e-money and ease with which e-money could be used which would again depend upon willingness of merchants to accept e-money. In other words, apart from security, privacy and ease, network effects are also important for wider use of e-money.

An economy like India, where cash transactions are very high, could benefit from using e-money through cost savings from printing and minting of smaller denomination notes and coins and eliminating the cost of handling, storing, transporting and insuring currency. These should also improve operational efficiency of the financial sector as also extension of banking to the urban poor and rural communities besides facilitating e-governance initiatives of governments. However, such benefits should be weighed against the need to build up the costly infrastructure to operate nationwide cashless retail payment system.

9.1.3 Implications of E-money for the Central Bank: Before analysing the likely implications, it is instructive to note that e-money can be issued in three alternate ways. Each of these three ways may have different implications for conduct of monetary policy.

1. E-money can be issued in exchange of cash (i.e. 100 percent backing of central bank money). Under that circumstance, there may be only marginal change in total money supply in the economy provided there is no significant change in velocity of circulation of money.
2. E-money can also be issued on credit against interest payment.
3. E-money could also be issued as a separate form of currency independent of central bank money by entities other than the central bank. In that case, e-money would compete against the central bank money as a medium of

exchange. However, such a scenario in which public gets e-money from an entity in exchange for something other than the central bank money seems remote now.

Currency notes and coins generally form an overwhelming part of the balance sheet of any central bank. If e-money is extensively used and in the process, replaces substantially central bank's money, central bank's balance sheet would *shrink* while that of the issuing authority of e-money would *expand* in relative terms.

With large scale use of e-money, it is apprehended that central bank's balance sheet may shrink to such an extent relative to that of the banking sector that it may be unable to perform its liquidity absorption function [in effect, open market operations (OMOs)] on account of non-availability of adequate volume of assets. Under that circumstance, extensive e-monetisation in the economy could jeopardise the conduct of monetary policy of the central bank. It may, however, be noted that the central bank would not have any problem in liquidity injection because central bank money is still the only legal tender in the economy.

Apart from constraining its liquidity management function, relative shrinkage in balance sheet may also have implications regarding loss of *seigniorage* revenue for the central bank. This is because currency notes and coins are the interest-free liability of the central bank towards public (i.e. public have in effect lent to the central bank such amount free of interest) which are then used by the central bank to purchase interest bearing assets. Thus, interest earned on these assets constitutes its seigniorage revenue. Therefore, if the central bank's operating costs are high which are more likely in an environment where central bank is required to intervene more, it may even incur losses on account of seigniorage revenue foregone. This may also have adverse implications for governments with chronic budget deficits as they would be deprived of the transfer of surplus to its treasury from the profitable central bank.

A distinguishing characteristic of e-money is that unlike

innovations in other retail payments media—which facilitate more efficient access to traditional form of central bank money—e-money could have the potential to become an independent medium of exchange. In that eventuality, two extreme views are being offered. On the one hand, one group perceives that in a highly technologically-advanced networked world, private entities may not require central bank money for settlement and, therefore, there may not be any central bank in future. Some of them also question whether private money is more efficient than central bank money from social welfare viewpoint and if so under what circumstance private money can replace central bank money altogether. On the other hand, there is another group of academicians and practitioners who strongly believe that central banks would continue to be as effective as ever though they may be required to respond differently in the changed environment.

9.1.4 E-money in India: In India, where cash transactions are high in number, the use of e-money can be beneficial in terms of reduced miscellaneous costs, viz. cost of printing and minting of smaller denomination notes and coins and transportation and storage costs. However, certain additional costs for setting up of network infrastructure to operate nationwide are also associated with it. The RBI has been partnering a multi-application smart card project, under the aegis of the Ministry of Communications and Information Technology, Government of India, to run a pilot project on the use of multi-application smart cards in the country. Various issues relating to technology, security, regulatory and supervisory concerns and legal implications have been examined to make the use of smart cards a viable proposition after the conclusion of the pilot project. The project is aimed at combining applications relating to banking, insurance, postal services, identification, etc. in a single card.

The Reserve Bank of India had constituted a Working Group on Electronic Money (Chairman: Zaire J. Camas) in January 2002 which submitted its Report in July 2002. The

Group identified certain areas of concern from the point of view of the central bank in the context of more widespread use of e-money. Some of the suggestions made by the Group included: (a) multi-purpose e-money to be issued only by authorised banks on a credit basis which should be strictly regulated and closely monitored, (b) redeemability should be ensured in order to preserve the unit of account function of money as well as to control money supply in the economy, and (c) reporting of e-money statistics should be ensured for the purposes of monetary policy and protection against criminal abuse such as money laundering.

9.2 E-money and Digital Money

Digital money (or *digital currency*) can be defined as an Internet-based form of currency or medium of exchange which is distinct from physical currency (banknotes and coins), but allows for instantaneous transactions and borderless transfer-of-ownership. Both virtual currencies and crypto_currencies are types of digital currencies, but the converse is incorrect. Like traditional money these currencies may be used to buy physical goods and services but could also be restricted to certain communities such as for example for use inside an on-line game or social network.

According to the Bank for International Settlements', "Digital Currencies" report of November 2015, digital currency is an asset represented in digital form and having some monetary characteristics. Digital currency can be denominated to a sovereign currency and issued by the issuer responsible to redeem digital money for cash. In that case, digital currency represents electronic money (e-money). Digital currency denominated in its own units of value or with decentralized or automatic issuance will be considered as a virtual currency.

Most of the traditional money supply is bank money held on computers. This is also considered digital currency. One could argue that our increasingly cashless society means that all currencies are becoming digital (sometimes referred to as *electronic money*), but they are not presented to us as such.

9.2.1 Types of Digital Currency:

A. Virtual Currency: According to the European Central Banks', "Virtual Currency Schemes: A Further Analysis" report of February 2015, virtual currency is a digital representation of value, not issued by a central bank, credit institution or e-money institution, which, in some circumstances, can be used as an alternative to money. In the previous report of October 2012, the virtual currency was defined as a type of unregulated, digital money, which is issued and usually controlled by its developers, and used and accepted among the members of a specific virtual community.

The US Department of Treasury in 2013 defined virtual currency more tersely as "a medium of exchange that operates like a currency in some environments, but does not have all the attributes of real currency". According to these definitions, virtual currency does not have the status of a legal tender.

B. Crypto Currency: A crypto currency is a type of digital token that relies on cryptography for chaining together digital signatures of token transfers, peer-to-peer networking and decentralization. In some cases, a proof-of-work scheme is used to create and manage the currency.

9.3 Electronic Commerce (E-commerce)

9.3.1 Types and Categories of E-commerce: E-commerce involves individuals and business organizations exchanging business information and instructions over electronic media using computers, telephones and other telecommunication equipments. Such form of doing business has been in existence ever since electronic mode of data/information exchange was developed, but its scope was limited only as a medium of exchange of information between entities with a pre-established contractual relationship. However, internet has changed the approach to e-commerce; it is no longer the same business with an additional channel for information exchange, but one with new strategy and models.

A business model generally focuses on: (a) where the business operates, i.e. the market, the competitors and the customers, (b) what it sells, i.e. its products and services, (c) the channels of distribution, i.e. the medium for sale and distribution of its products, and (d) the sources of revenue and expenditure and how these are affected. Internet has influenced all the four components of business model and thus has come to influence the business strategy in a profound way. The size of the market has grown enormously as one can access the products and services from any part of the world. So does the potential competition. The methods of reaching out to customers, receiving the response and offering services have a new, simpler and efficient alternative now, i.e. internet. The cost of advertisement, offer and delivery of services through internet has reduced considerably, forcing most companies to rework their strategies to remain in competition.

There are two types of e-commerce ventures in operation: (a) the old brick and mortar companies, who have adopted electronic medium, particularly internet, to enhance their existing products and services, and/or to offer new products and services, and (b) the pure e-ventures who have no visible physical presence. This difference has wider ramifications than mere visibility when it comes to issues like customer's trust, brand equity, ability to service the customers, adopting new business culture and cost.

Another way of classifying e-commerce is by the targeted counterpart of a business, viz. whether the counterpart is a final consumer or another business in the distribution chain. Accordingly, the two broad categories are: business-to-consumer (B2C) and business-to-business (B2B).

9.3.2 Business-to-Consumers (B2C): In the B2C category are included single e-shops, shopping malls, e-broking, e-auction, e-banking, service providers like travel related services, financial services, education, entertainment and any other form of business targeted at the final consumer. Some of the features, opportunities and concerns common to this category of business irrespective of the business segment, are the following.

Internet provides an ever-growing market both in terms of number of potential customers and geographical reach. Technological development has made access to internet both cheaper and faster. More and more people across the globe are accessing the net either through PCs or other devices. The purchasing power and need for quality service of this segment of consumers are considerable. Anybody accessing Internet is a potential customer irrespective of his or her location. Thus, any business targeting final consumers cannot ignore the business potential of Internet.

Internet offers a unique opportunity to register business presence in a global market. Its effectiveness in disseminating information about one's business at a relatively cost effective manner is tremendous. Time sensitive information can be updated faster than any other media. A properly designed website can convey a more accurate and focussed image of a product or service than any other media. Use of multimedia capabilities, i.e. sound, picture, movies etc. has made internet as an ideal medium for information dissemination. However, help of other media is necessary to draw the potential customers to the web site.

The quality of service is a key feature of any e-commerce venture. The ability to sell one's product at anytime and anywhere to the satisfaction of customers is essential for e-business to succeed. Internet offers such opportunity, since the business presence is not restricted by time zone and geographical limitations. Replying to customers' queries through e-mail, offering interactive help line, accepting customers' complaints online 24 hours a day and attending to the same etc. are some of the features of e-business which enhance the quality of service to the customers. It is of crucial importance for an e-venture to realize that just as it is easier to approach a customer through internet, it is equally easy to lose him. The customer has the same facility to move over to another site.

Cost is an important issue in an e-venture. It is generally

accepted that the cost of overhead, servicing and distribution etc. through internet is less compared to the traditional way of doing business. Although the magnitude of difference varies depending on the type of business and the estimates made, but there is unanimity that Internet provides a substantial cost advantage and this, in fact, is one of the major driving forces for more number of traditional business adopting to e-commerce and pure e-commerce firms to sprout.

Cost of communication through www is the least compared to any other medium. Many a time one's presence in the web may bring in international enquiries, which the business might not have targeted. The business should have proper plans to address such opportunities.

There are various obstacles, which an e-commerce venture needs to overcome. Trust of customers in a web venture is an important concern. Many customers hesitate to deal with a web venture as they are not sure of the type of products and services they will receive. This is particularly true in a B2C venture like e-shop, e-mall or e-auction site. Traditional business with well-established brands and goodwill and having a physical presence face less resistance from customers in this regard than a pure e-venture.

Many B2C ventures have ultimately to deliver a product or service in physical form to the customer for a deal contracted through internet. This needs proper logistics, an efficient distribution network, and control over quality of product or service delivered. These issues are not technology related and any let off in this area can drive the customer away to the competitor or from e-commerce.

The privacy of information on the customer's preferences, credit card and bank account details etc. and customers' faith in a system where such privacy is stated to be ensured are important issues to be addressed. These are mainly technological issues, but human factor is important both at the business and at the customers' end and also in building the trust in the system.

Security of a transaction, authenticity of a deal, identification of a customer etc. are important technological and systems issues, which are major sources of concern to e-commerce. Equally important are questions of repudiation of a deal, applicability of law, jurisdiction of tax laws etc. These are important to all forms of e-commerce, whether B2C or B2B and all segments of business, i.e. manufacturing, services and finance. Accessibility to Internet by the consumers is an important issue in B2C domain. This is particularly so in countries like India where penetration of PCs and other devices to households for access to Internet is minimal. Also important are availability of bandwidth and other infrastructure for faster and easier access. Considering that e-commerce aims at global market, deficiencies of these kinds in the developing world are no longer concerns confined to these areas, but are global e-commerce concerns.

9.3.3 Business to Business (B2B): As opposed to B2C e-commerce, in B2B domain, the parties to a deal are at different points of the product supply chain. In a B2B type domain, a company, its suppliers, dealers and bankers are networked to finalize and settle all aspects of a deal online. Perhaps, only the goods in different stages of processing physically move from the supplier to the dealer. This scenario can be extended to include the shipper, providers of different ancillary services, IT service provider and the payment system gateway etc. depending on the degree of sophistication of the available systems.

Another important feature of a B2B domain, as distinct from B2C, is that business information/data is integrated to the back office systems of parties to a deal and the state of straight through processing (STP) or near STP is achieved. This is a very significant aspect of B2B model of e-commerce, which results in improved profits through lowering cost and reducing inventories.

For example, in a B2B environment, the back office system of a company controls inventory requirement with reference to the order book position updated regularly on the basis of orders received from dealers through internet. At the optimum level of inventory, it raises a purchase order with the supplier, whose system, in turn, processes the order and confirms supply. Buyer company's system issues debit instructions on its bank account for payment to the supplier. The buyer's bank credits seller's bank with the cost of sale though a payment gateway. Similar series of transaction processes are also initiated between the company and its dealers and their respective banks. Once e-commerce relationship is established between the firms, the transactions of the type shown above can be processed with minimal human intervention and on 24 hours a day and 7 day a week basis.

New business models are emerging in B2B domain. There are portals which offer a meeting ground to buyers and sellers of different products in supply chain, more like a buyer-seller meet in international business. This has enabled relatively smaller companies to enter the global market. Banks in the portal offer financial services for deals settled through the portal.

Technology and networking are important constituents of a B2B type of business domain. Earlier, only large firms could have access to such technology and they used private networks with interface to each other for information flow and transaction processing. A major concern used to be compatibility of EDI platforms across different B2B partners. Internet with www and other standard technology have offered opportunity to relatively smaller and medium sized firms to integrate their operations in B2B model and take advantage of the benefits it offers. It has also led to standardization of software platforms.

Other new forms of business models in B2B domain are application service providers (ASPs) and service integrators. ASPs offer application software online to e-commerce companies who pay for the same according to the use without owning it. Often entire back office processing is taken care of by ASPs and other service integrators. However, the utility of such service providers will to a large extent depend on the business strategy of the e-venture.

The concerns of B2B e-commerce are similar to those of B2C, discussed earlier. The security issues are more pronounced because of high value transfers taking place through the net. So also are the issues relating to privacy of information, law, tax repudiation etc. The other issues of importance to a B2B firm are the choice of appropriate technology, the issue of build or outsource, maintenance and training of personnel etc., since they involve large investments and are critical to success.

9.4 Internet Marketing

New forms of marketing also use the internet and are therefore called *internet marketing* or more generally *e-marketing, online marketing, digital marketing*. Internet marketing is sometimes considered to be broad in scope, because it not only refers to marketing on the internet, but also includes marketing done via e-mail, wireless media as well as driving audience from traditional marketing methods like radio and billboard to internet properties or landing page.

E-marketing (electronic marketing) can be described as the marketing of the company's products that occurs over the internet and mobile. The objective behind performing electronic marketing is to increase the awareness of a particular company amongst the consumer market. E-marketing is a novel form of marketing which has been developed in conjunction with the ever-growing popularity of the internet and website marketing. Being a relatively new form of marketing in India, majority of corporations continue to market themselves with use of the traditional methods of print magazine advertisements and television commercials.

Many companies, who are experts in website marketing and have been conducting business operations over the internet for a couple of years, are aware of electronic marketing and the amazing results in business success it can quickly and effortlessly achieve for them.

The growth of the internet during the past few years is undoubtedly the most important development in the history of commerce which shows no signs of abating in the future. Since the Industrial Revolution of the 19th century, no development has so dramatically altered human behaviour as the emergence of internet. Marketing has also been immensely influenced by the internet. Marketers have got a new medium for communicating and building long-term relationship with their customers at a fraction of cost they used to incur earlier. Various marketing activities can be performed more efficiently, effectively and smoothly than ever before with the help of internet. However, it is difficult to assess the potential of internet for business and foresee the probable threats brought by the new medium.

In India, the internet became available to the general public and the business in 1995. People have been mesmerized by the prowess of the internet, both as a communication tool and as an entertainment medium. The Indian corporate world was quick to realise the commercial potential of the web and embraced it as part of its business and marketing strategies. The Indian Government has also been providing the necessary infrastructural support for the internet. Worldwide, and in India also, empirical studies are being conducted to explore the possibilities of doing business on the internet, including growth in the volume of e-commerce, use of websites, on-line pricing and online advertising. However, what marketers in India think about the internet as a marketing tool and how they can use it for marketing purposes has not been attempted in a systematic manner.

10

Digital Technology for Pradhan Mantri Jan-Dhan Yojana (PMJDY), 2014

The efforts to include the financially excluded segments of the society in India are not new. The concept was first mooted by the Reserve Bank of India in 2005 and branchless banking through banking agents called *Bank Mitras* [Business Correspondents (BCs)] was started in the year 2006. In the year 2011, banks covered 74,351 villages, with population more than 2,000 (as per 2001 census), with banking facilities under the *Swabhimaan* campaign. However, the programme had a very limited reach and impact.

This campaign was limited in its approach in terms of reach and coverage. Convergence of various aspects of comprehensive financial inclusion like opening of bank accounts, access to digital money, availing of micro credit, insurance and pension was lacking. The campaign focused only on the supply side by providing banking facility in villages of population greater than 2,000 but the entire geography was not targeted. There was no focus on the households. Also some technology issues hampered further scalability of the campaign. Consequently the desired benefits could not be achieved and a large number of bank accounts remained dormant. A comprehensive plan was felt necessary to keep the accounts active and use them as an instrument of some economic activity leading to livelihoods.

In order to provide the much needed thrust, a flagship programme called the Pradhan Mantri Jan-Dhan Yojana was announced by the Prime Minister in his Independence Day address to the nation on August 15, 2014. PMJDY was launched on August 28, 2014, across the country simultaneously. PMJDY lies at the core of development philosophy of *Sab Ka Sath Sab Ka*

Vikas (inclusive growth).

10.1 PMJDY: Brief Introduction

PMJDY is a National Mission on financial inclusion. This Mission would enable all households, urban and rural, to gain easy and universal access to financial services. In this Mission, households will not only have bank accounts with indigenous RuPay debit cards but will also gain access to credit for economic activity and to insurance and pension services for their social security. The Mission has a strong focus on the use of technology and incorporates lessons learnt from earlier efforts.

PMJDY encompasses an integrated approach to bring about comprehensive financial inclusion of all the households in the country. The plan envisages universal access to banking facilities with at least one basic banking account for every household, financial literacy, access to credit, insurance and pension facility. In addition, the beneficiaries would get RuPay debit card having in-built accident insurance cover of ₹ 1 lakh. The plan also envisages channelling all Government benefits (from Centre/State/Local Body) to the beneficiaries' accounts and pushing the Direct Benefits Transfer (DBT) scheme of the Union Government. The technological issues like poor connectivity, online transactions will be addressed. Mobile transactions through telecom operators and their established centres as cash out points are also planned to be used for financial inclusion under the Scheme. Also an effort is being made to reach out to the youth of the country to participate in this Mission Mode Programme.

PMJDY aims to provide bank account to every household in the country and make available the following basic banking services facilities:

- Opening of bank account with RuPay debit card and mobile banking facility.
- Cash withdrawal and deposits.
- Transfer.

- Balance enquiry.
- Mini statement.

Other services are also to be provided in due course in a time-bound manner apart from financial literacy which is to be disseminated side by side to make citizens capable to use optimum utilization of available financial services. To provide these banking services banking outlets to be provided within 5 kilometres distance of every village. Necessary infrastructure also needs to be placed to enable e-KYC for account opening and AEPS for withdrawal of cash based biometric authentication from UIDAI database.

10.2 Six Pillars of PMJDY

PMJDY, to be executed in the Mission Mode, envisages provision of affordable financial services to all citizens within a reasonable distance. It comprises of the following six pillars:

1. **Universal Access to Banking Facilities:** Mapping of each district into sub-service area (SSA) catering to 1,000-1,500 households in a manner that every habitation has access to banking services within a reasonable distance say 5 km. by August 14, 2015. Coverage of parts of J&K, Himachal Pradesh, Uttarakhand, North-East and the Left wing extremism affected districts which have telecom connectivity and infrastructure constraints would spill over to the Phase II of the program (August 15, 2015 to August 15, 2018).

2. **Providing Basic Banking Accounts with Overdraft Facility and RuPay Debit Card to all Households:** The effort would be to first cover all uncovered households with banking facilities by August, 2015, by opening basic bank accounts. Account holder would be provided a RuPay debit card. Facility of an overdraft to every basic banking account holder would be considered after satisfactory operation/credit history of six months.

3. **Financial Literacy Programme:** Financial literacy would be an integral part of the Mission in order to let the beneficiaries make best use of the financial services being

made available to them.

4. **Creation of Credit Guarantee Fund:** Creation of a Credit Guarantee Fund would be to cover the defaults in overdraft accounts.

5. **Micro Insurance:** To provide micro-insurance to all willing and eligible persons by August 14, 2018, and then on an ongoing basis.

6. **Unorganized Sector Pension Schemes like Swavalamban:** By August 14, 2018 and then on an ongoing basis.

10.3 Challenges Identified in Implementing the Mission

10.3.1 Telecom Connectivity: The feedback from the banks is that in tribal and hilly areas of the country, the telecom network is not reliable and therefore setting up *Bank Mitra* (Business Correspondent) in these areas and ensuring opening of bank accounts is going to be difficult. A meeting was held with the representatives of the Department of Telecom (DoT) and BSNL in this regard and it was assured that the ongoing telecom connectivity problems would be resolved by mutual consultation. It was also informed that DoT is separately seeking the Government approval to cover all villages in the North-East and difficult areas with telecom connectivity. Banks would also work to utilize the National Optical Fibre Network (NOFN) when it reaches the panchayat level.

10.3.2 Keeping the Accounts Live: It is essential that all Government benefits—Central, State or local—should flow to these accounts as it has been observed that a lot of duplicity exists in this area and sometimes States have not followed the service area approach and allocated areas to some banks other than service area banks creating avoidable confusion. The DBT schemes especially MNREGA need to be pushed and DBT in LPG needs to be restarted.

10.3.3 Brand Awareness and Sensitization: In order to achieve a "demand" side pull effect, it would be essential that there is branding and awareness on *Bank Mitra* (Business

Correspondent) model for providing basic banking services, banking products available at *Bank Mitra* (Business Correspondent) outlets and RuPay cards. Customers to be made aware that overdraft of up to ₹ 5,000 to be provided in their account is a credit facility which needs to be repaid in order to get fresh limits and is not a grant.

10.3.4 Commission to Bank on Direct Benefit Transfer (DBT): A task force on Aadhaar-enabled Unified Payment infrastructure headed by Sh. Nandan Nilekani in its report in February 2012 recommended that last mile transaction cost of 3.14 percent with a cap of ₹ 20 per transaction be budgeted for various EBT, DTS and last mile payments through Micro-ATMs and ATMs. The commission applicable for DBT should also cover DBTL (DBT of LPG). MGNREGA may also be included in the Direct Benefit Transfer.

10.3.5 Coverage of Difficult Areas: Parts of North-East, Himachal Pradesh, Uttarakhand, J&K and 82 Left wing extremism (LWE) districts face challenges of infrastructure besides telecom connectivity. All households in such areas may not be fully covered under the campaign.

Coverage of some of the areas might, therefore, spill over to Phase-II.

10.4 Roles of Major Stakeholders

10.4.1 Department of Financial Services:

- Overall ownership of the Mission Mode Project on Financial Inclusion.
- Overall monitoring and implementation of the Mission.

10.4.2 Other Central Government Departments:

- In order to achieve the complete financial inclusion and transfer of social benefits in the accounts of the beneficiaries, the concerned Departments of Central Government would coordinate with the stake holders.
- Presently, 26 centrally social benefits scheme under DBT are sponsored by 8 Departments of the Central Government as under:

1. Ministry of Social Justice and Empowerment.
2. Ministry of Human Resources Development, d/o Higher Education.
3. Ministry of Human Resources Development, d/o School Education and Literacy.
4. Ministry of Tribal Affairs.
5. Ministry of Minority Affairs.
6. Ministry of Women and Child Development.
7. Ministry of Health and Family Welfare.
8. Ministry of Labour and Employment.

- MGNREGA is sponsored by Ministry of Rural Development (MoRD, GoI), and is likely to be included in Direct Benefit Transfer.
- Department of Posts for using the rural post offices, *Gramin Dak Sewak*, Department of Telecommunications for telecom connectivity, Ministry of Information and Broadcasting and DAVP to assist in media campaign, DEITY in development of logistic support for monitoring like creation of portal for data updating, development of electronic reporting system, MoRD for convergence with NRLM, HUPA for convergence with NULM etc.

10.4.3 Reserve Bank of India (RBI):
- To align their directions to the banks on financial inclusion with the Mission Mode.
- FIF fund allocation support.
- Depositor Education and Awareness Fund Scheme, 2014 support.
- To guide and support banks in financial literacy campaign and revamping and expansion of FLCCs upto the block level.

10.4.4 Indian Banks' Association (IBA):
- Coordination in financial inclusion effort with all banks.
- Key monitoring role in financial literacy campaign.
- Coordination in publicity and campaign.
- Coordination in centralised handling of customer grievances through toll-free numbers in coordination with banks.
- A dedicated desk to be set up for monitoring and

implementation of FI. Coordinate with SLBC for grievance redressal.

10.4.5 National Bank for Agriculture and Rural Development (NABARD):

- Coordination in publicity and campaign.
- Monitoring of implementation of financial inclusion in respect of organisations working under NABARD.
- Allocation of funds from Financial Inclusion Fund (FIF).
- Financial literacy by SHGs/JLGs beneficiaries.

10.4.6 State Governments:

- Appointment of Mission director at the State level.
- Monitoring of financial inclusion campaign in coordination with SLBC and all the stake holders.
- Direct Benefit Transfer of the State schemes in the bank accounts of the beneficiaries.
- One officer of the State Government on deputation to oversee implementation issue.

10.4.7 Local Bodies:

- Representatives of local bodies (panchayats in rural areas and municipalities in urban areas) to assist in implementation of financial inclusion in various ways like in organising camps in opening of accounts, identification of persons for opening of account, in financial literacy campaign etc.

10.4.8 National Payment Corporation of India (NPCI):

- Coordination and necessary guidance and supports to banks for in providing and proper operations of RuPay cards.
- To facilitate inter-operability among *Bank Mitras* (Business Correspondents).
- Necessary supports to banks in making available USSD-based mobile banking with low-end mobile phones so that customers can avail basic banking services like deposits, withdrawals, funds transfer, balance enquiry etc. across the banks. This product may be enabled at *Bank Mitra* (Business Correspondent) outlets also.

10.4.9 Unique Identification Authority of India (UIDAI):

- Convergence of Aadhaar enrolment with bank account

opening.

- Facilitating the subsidy scheme on procurement of Aadhaar-enabled Payment System (AEPS) machines by banks.
- Fast conversion of EID to UID to ensure faster credit to bank accounts.
- Mapping multiple accounts with a single Aadhaar number.

10.5 Use of Digital Technology for PMJDY, 2014

PMJDY, under National Mission on Financial Inclusion, proposes to use the technology in a big way to achieve the goal in a time-bound manner. Some of the major products are explained hereunder:

10.5.1 Electronically Know Your Customer (e-KYC): In the year 2013, RBI permitted e-KYC as a valid process for KYC verification under Prevention of Money Laundering (Maintenance of Records) Rules, 2005. In order to reduce the risk of identity fraud, documentary forgery and have paperless KYC verification, UIDAI has launched its e-KYC services. Under the e-KYC process—and after the explicit consent of the customer and after his or her biometric authentication from UIDAI data base—individual basic data comprising name, age, gender and photograph can be shared electronically with authorised users like banks, which is a valid process for KYC.

The aforesaid process is paperless and has made the account opening of customers having Aadhaar number much easier. Almost all the banks have either adopted this process or are in the advance stage of putting the system live. The e-KYC process would be used in large scale for opening accounts in future.

10.5.2 Transaction through Mobile Banking: The mobile phone revolution that is transforming the country could also turn into a banking revolution in terms of reach and transaction. The reach of mobile to the remote village and its usage by the common man has become order of the day and it is estimated that around 1/4th of mobile users are residing in villages/small towns. The coverage of mobile phones and the use of such instruments by all sections of the population can be exploited for extending financial services to the excluded population. It enables the subscribers to manage their financial transactions (funds transfer) independent of place and time. The subscriber can approach a retailer of mobile network for withdrawal/deposit of money and the transaction takes place using SMS messages.

The mobile banking services are generally available through a java application on Blackberry, Android, iPhones and Windows mobile phones. Various banking services like funds transfer, immediate payment services, enquiry services (balance enquiry/mini-statement), demat account services, requests for cheque book, bill payments etc. may be carried out through mobile banking. There are transaction limits for mobile banking and these services are free of charge. The mobile banking services are also available over SMS.

The basic financial transactions from the bank accounts can be executed through a mobile based PIN system using mobile banking. Mobile banking through mobile wallet was also launched in 2012. Mobile telephony and pre-paid wallets can also be utilized for coverage of households under the financial inclusion campaign.

10.5.3 Immediate Payment System (IMPS): IMPS was launched by NPCI on November 22, 2010. It offers an instant, 24x7, inter-bank electronic fund transfer service through mobile phones as well as internet banking and ATMs. In the process of remittances across the bank there are four stakeholders, i.e.: (a) remitter (sender), (b) beneficiary (receiver), (c) banks, and (d) National Financial Switch.

In order to remit fund through IMPS, the sender should use mobile banking to send money, the receiver mobile number should be registered with his bank and the money is credited to receivers account instantly. For registration, the remitter must register for mobile banking and get mobile money identifier (MMID) and mobile banking PIN (MPIN) for initiation of a transaction. MMID is a 7-digit number, to be issued by the bank to the customer upon registration and the beneficiary must register his/her mobile number with the bank account and get MMID. A remitter can initiate an IMPS transaction by sending an SMS to his bank typing the beneficiary mobile number, beneficiary MMID and amount. The receiver will get an SMS confirmation for the credit of his account. National Payments Corporation of India (NPCI) is facilitating the inter-bank mobile payment service (IMPS).

10.5.4 Micro-ATMs: Micro-ATMs are biometric authentication enabled hand-held devices. In order to make the ATMs viable at rural/semi-urban centres, low cost Micro-ATMs can be deployed at each of the *Bank Mitra* (Business Correspondent) location. This would enable a person to instantly deposit or withdraw funds regardless of the bank associated with a particular *Bank Mitra*. This device can be based on a mobile phone connection and made available to every *Bank Mitra* (Business Correspondent). Customers would have to get their identity authenticated and withdraw or put money into their bank accounts. This money will come from the cash drawer of the *Bank Mitra*. Essentially, *Bank Mitras* will act as bank for the customers and all they need to do is verify the authenticity of customer using customer's UID. The basic transaction types to be supported by micro-ATMs are deposit, withdrawal, fund transfer and balance enquiry. Micro-ATM offers one of the most promising options for providing financial services to the unbanked population. Micro-ATMs would have various options of authentication like biometric, PIN-based etc. and they can also be used as mobile ATMs to enable transactions near the door step of the customers.

Micro-ATMs offer an online interoperable, low-cost payments platform to everyone in the country.

10.5.5 National Unified USSD Platform (NUUP): Mobile banking is one of the most potent modes for increasing reach of banking facilities to the masses. Today, mobile phones have become a household device in India.

Mobile banking service can be initiated using SMS—an unencrypted service, considered unsafe—or using mobile banking app. Though very interactive, the major problem with mobile banking apps is that these need to be downloaded and installed on the mobile phone. Less than 40 percent of Indian users have compatible J2ME handsets and GPRS connection on their mobile phone, as required by this system.

To resolve aforesaid issues, an alternative solution on USSD platform is available. Customers can avail USSD solution through any mobile phone on GSM network, irrespective of make and model of the phone. This does not require any application to be downloaded on customer's mobile phone and need for GPRS connectivity. USSD is user-friendly so it is easy to communicate and educate customers as well. USSD alleviates the need for application download and is more secure than SMS channel.

Banking customers can use this service by dialling *99#, a "Common number across all Telecom Service Providers, (TSPs)", on their mobile and transact through an interactive menu displayed on the mobile screen.

Using *99#, a customer will be able to access both financial services (like funds transfer) and non-financial services (like balance enquiry and mini-statement of bank account), at his/her own convenience. Key services that NUUP will offer include inter-bank account to account funds transfer, balance enquiry, mini-statement besides host of other services. A notable inclusion in the NUUP service is a new addition in the form of Query Service on Aadhaar Mapper (QSAM). Under this feature, a user can come to know about his/her Aadhaar seeding status with the banks, a service that will find tremendous utility for the government's direct subsidy disbursals programme. This product was scheduled to be launched on August 28, 2014.

10.5.6 RuPay Debit Cards: RuPay is a new card payment scheme launched by the National Payments Corporation of India (NPCI), to offer a domestic, open-loop, multilateral system which will allow all Indian banks and financial institutions in India to participate in electronic payments.

'RuPay', the word itself has a sense of nationality in it. RuPay is the coinage of two terms Rupee and Payment. RuPay cards address the needs of Indian consumers, merchants and banks. The benefits of RuPay debit card include the flexibility of the product platform, high levels of acceptance and the strength of the RuPay brand, all of which will contribute to an increased product experience. The main features are: (a) lower cost and affordability, (b) customized product offering, (c) protection of information related to Indian consumers, and (d) provides electronic product options to untapped/unexplored consumer segment.

10.5.7 Aadhaar-enabled Payment System (AEPS): AEPS is a banking product which allows online interoperable financial inclusion transaction at PoS (micro-ATM) or kiosk banking through the Business Correspondent of any bank using the Aadhaar authentication. Presently, four Aadhaar-enabled basic types of banking transactions are available, i.e.: (a) balance enquiry, (b) cash withdrawal, (c) cash deposit and (d) Aadhaar to Aadhaar funds transfer. For undertaking AEPS transaction by customer, two inputs, i.e. IIN (Identifying the Bank to which the customer is associated) and Aadhaar number are required.

10.5.8 Aadhaar Payments Bridge System (APBS): APBS enables the transfer of payments from Government and Government Institutions to Aadhaar-enabled accounts of beneficiaries at banks and post offices. Every Government Department or Institution that sends EBT and DBT/DBTL payments to individuals simply needs to prepare a file containing the Aadhaar number and amount and submit it to their accredited bank. The accredited bank then processes the file through an interoperable Aadhaar payments bridge and funds are credited into the accounts of beneficiaries. Upon receiving incoming funds, the beneficiary's bank will notify him or her through an SMS or any other communication channel that is established between the bank and the customer.

To sum up, PMJDY is a National Mission on financial

inclusion to provide all households in the country with financial services, with particular focus to empower the weaker sections of society, including women, small and marginal farmers and labourers, both rural and urban. The necessity of launching such a mission was felt in view of the fact that less than two-thirds of the households in the country have access to banking facilities even after 70 years of Independence. The Mission seeks to provide all households in the country, both rural and urban, with access to the financial services, like bank account with RuPay debit card, access to credit, remittance, insurance and pension. Thus, the Mission not only brings the excluded sections into the financial mainstream but makes the transfer of benefits of various subsidy schemes of the government more efficient.

11

Digital Services in Agriculture and Rural Development

11.1 Need for IT-based Services to Farmers

Various sectors of the Indian economy such as industry, finance, insurance, communications and transport have adopted information technology in a big way. However, agricultural sector of the economy is lagging behind in utilizing IT services. Some efforts have been made in this regard but they are by no means adequate. The rapid strides that the country has registered in the IT field will remain incomplete unless IT is fully utilised to ensure more efficient and productive Indian agriculture. Practically there is no area in agriculture in which IT has no role to play. The immense scale and diversity of Indian agriculture provides the ultimate challenge to the potential of information technology.

The adoption of IT services in agriculture depends on the main functionaries involved in Indian agriculture. These functionaries can make a big contribution to the growth of agriculture with the assistance of IT. For this purpose, the following functionaries can be considered: (a) farmers, (b) industries providing inputs to agriculture, (c) industries dealing with agricultural output, (d) central and state governments, and (e) NGOs working for the benefit of farmers and agricultural universities and research centres.

Indian farmers, for whose welfare, a huge government machinery is devoted, still suffer from the absence of right information at the required time. The farmers require timely information on weather conditions, sowing time, availability of inputs including credit, expert advice on maintaining crops in healthy conditions, information on markets and on all other areas of interest to them.

In spite of the best efforts and expenditure, the conventional apparatus has not been able to deliver the goods satisfactorily. Herein, lies the role of IT which can efficiently address the concerns of farmers stationed at even remote locations. Low literacy levels, cost of computers, poor communication infrastructure make it impossible for individual farmers, particularly small farmers, to directly adopt IT. This calls for institutional efforts to provide IT-based services to farmers.

In order to keep pace with the state-of-the-art technologies, National Informatics Centre (NIC) has been conducting various training programmes on IT application on a regular basis from time to time for the user organisations of agriculture sector. Agricultural Informatics Division of NIC has taken up various initiatives in bringing IT-led development which includes Web-enabled applications, GIS-based applications, multimedia applications, database applications and e-governance and training.

11.2 Rural Portal of Ministry of Rural Development (MoRD)

MoRD has developed a number of applications to automate the processes of information generation and strengthening E-governance. Efforts have also been made to develop national level ICT solutions for some important activities like the land records computerization, MIS for Mahatma Gandhi National Rural Employment Guarantee Act (MGNREGA) and, online monitoring of schemes like Rural Bazaar, RuralSoft.

Rural Portal provides a gateway to around 150 websites. It provides details of schemes of the Ministry, their physical and financial status, release position, sanction orders etc. Apart from this, news related to Ministry is also uploaded daily onto the site. Circulars of public interest, information regarding events, tenders/notices, e-mail are also uploaded regularly onto the site. Online SARAS Mela is available on the website to web showcase the products made by rural artisans for wide publicity and to create national/international market for their products. Applications have been developed to monitor online

Monthly Progress Reports of schemes of the Ministry.

NIC-DRD informatics cell has designed and developed the software for the household survey BPL Census 2002. The software was designed in such a way that it uniquely identifies a family and all the members of the family at national level. It also assigns a unique number to all panchayats which are the executing agencies/service providers for most of the schemes of MoRD. The family and the persons whose information is captured in the software are the beneficiary/service receiver for most of the schemes of MoRD and are uniquely identified.

11.3 National Rural Employment Guarantee Act Software Package (NREGASoft)

MoRD and NIC commenced the preparation of appropriate e-governance solution to strengthen NREGA in October 2005 and when the scheme was launched in February 2006, the NREGASoft was also launched across the country. The software is available to all stakeholders online through http://nrega.nic.in and also could be downloaded for off-line working. The package is unicode-enabled and supports local languages. The training to use the software has been organized in States.

NREGAsoft is web-based software prepared to capture all the activities under NREGA at National/State/District/Block and panchayat level. Using this portal each stakeholder can input information and access his/her own information through this portal. NREGAsoft captures Registration of workers, work demanded, number of days of employment for whole family, funds transferred/utilized and number of works undertaken under the scheme. Various stake holders of the project are the following:

1. Citizens.
2. Gram panchayats, block panchayats, and zilla panchayats.
3. Workers.
4. Programme officers.
5. District programme co-ordinators.

6. Implementing agencies other then PRIs.
7. State RD Departments.
8. Ministry of Rural Development and administrators in Government of India.

11.3.1 Various Modules of the Software: These are the following:

A. Beneficiary Management Module: It captures registration, demand for work, work allocation and muster rolls on which a person worked, the software has the provision of payment of wages through bank/post office as it captures the bank/post office account number, bank/post office name, branch name for all the person who demanded job and their account number are shown in muster roll against their name and calculate unemployment allowance, if any and also keep tracks of number of days of employment of a family.

B. Fund Management Module: It captures the funds transferred from MoRD/States to districts and then to programme officers/panchayats and expenditure incurred by various implementing agencies on labour, material and contingency. Hence, it keeps track of each and every paisa spent under the scheme.

C. Works Management Module: It captures information about the various works under taken under the scheme at various level. It facilitates online approval of projects and keeps track of time taken for approval of project. Each project is provided a unique ID and status of work is maintained in the system.

D. Grievance Redressal System: It allows a worker/citizen to lodge complaint and trace the subsequent response.

E. Staffing Position Module: It captures name, telephone numbers etc. of all the officials, planning and implementing agencies from gram panchayat to MoRD involved in NREGA, thus strengthening communication and coordination among them.

F. Alerts: The software also gives alerts to implementing agencies about the various irregularities, important activities, messages for funds to be received by the agencies.

G. Gram Panchayat Accounting System: NREGA put lot of responsibility on gram panchayats as registration, demand for work and allocation of work can be done only by gram panchayats. Software assists gram panchayats as follows:

1. It keeps track of 100 days of the employment to a family.
2. It ensures that a worker should not work on two worksites simultaneously.
3. The software keeps track of the fund released from the MoRD/States to the districts and then from districts to blocks/gram panchayats so it helps in reconciliation of accounts.
4. It provides status of available funds in the accounts at panchayats, blocks and districts levels.

11.4 IFFCO-ISRO Cooperation

IFFCO has initiated IT-based services for farmers and cooperative societies. It has taken up a project in association with Indian Space Research Organisation (ISRO) to utilise satellite based remote sensing data and geographical information systems (GIS). Developed countries have been utilising precision farming with the help of IT tools for a long time. While this will take a long time for our country due to small holdings, it is to be noted that GIS has an invaluable role to play even in the existing conditions. Remote sensing and GIS information can provide warnings on evolving crop stresses, crop vigour etc.

The IFFCO-ISRO GIS project extends support for efficient and timely availability of IFFCO's fertiliser to farmers though better logistics and efficient operations. Based on the experience gained from this project, more intensive services based on GIS are envisaged for the entire country. In addition to the GIS-based services, effort is being made to create databases that contain information of interest to the farmers. These include recommendation on package of practices for major cereals, pulses, horticulture, floriculture and animal husbandry etc. Information on various inputs such as seeds, fertilisers, credit is provided. An important service envisaged is to provide access to the nearest expert in case of stress or any other problem witnessed in the crops. Facilities are sought to be provided to encourage and share farm experiences by forging various crop forums. Many of the agricultural extension services are also proposed to be made online using multimedia facilities.

In order to encourage farmers to obtain best possible price, information regarding prices of various crops prevailing in approachable markets (*mandies*) is also being provided. Other areas of interest to farmers such as distance education, location specific news etc. are also planned.

11.5 Cyber Dhabas

To take IT to the door steps of the farmers, it is proposed that a large number of access points called cyber dhabas are setup. These cyber dhabas should be provided with a PC and a modem with telephone connection to connect to the databases. The farmers can take the assistance of the operator of cyber dhabas for a nominal charge. The major bottleneck in spreading e-culture to rural areas is related to connectivity i.e. ensuring that the access points can get connected to the databases which are in selected locations.

Since dialup lines are very slow, other viable options are required to be explored. Unfortunately, the alternatives are expensive and may not be feasible. One silver lining is that several private operators are connecting important cities with fibre optic which provides a very reliable and fast access. Since these will pass through rural areas, it is possible to explore the possibility of tapping this potential by laying the last mile connectivity. Once this is done, substantial segment of rural India can access the IT-based services.

11.6 E-choupal

E-choupal offers farmers the information, products and services they need to enhance productivity, improve farm-gate price realisation, and cut transaction costs. Farmers can access the latest local and global information on weather, scientific farming practices, as well as market prices at the village itself through this web portal—all in Hindi. E-choupal also facilitates the supply of high quality farm inputs as well as the purchase of commodities at the farm.

Given the literacy and infrastructure constraints at the village level, this model is designed to provide physical service support through a choupal sanchalak, himself a lead farmer, who acts as the interface between the system and the farmers. The contents of this site in their entirety are made available only to the registered sanchalaks.

11.7 E-panchayat

E-panchayat is one of the Mission Mode Project (MMP), currently being implemented with a vision to empower and transform rural India. As a first step towards formulating the project, the Ministry of Panchayati Raj constituted an Expert Group in June, 2007 under the Chairmanship of Dr. B.K. Gairola, Director General, NIC, Government of India. The Expert Group was entrusted with the task of assessing the IT Programmes of Ministry of Panchayati Raj and recommending cost effective solutions along with the cost implications. Adopting a consultative approach, the Committee interacted with the States/UTs to assess the existing status of computerization up to the Gram Panchayat level, including the initiatives undertaken by the State Governments. The recommendations of the Committee formed the basis for the conceptualization of E-Panchayat.

The E-panchayat project holds great promise for the rural masses as it aims to transform the panchayati raj institutions (PRIs) into symbols of modernity, transparency and efficiency. This is a one of its kind nationwide IT initiative introduced by Ministry of Panchayati Raj that endeavours to ensure people's participation in programme decision-making, implementation and delivery. The project aims to automate the functioning of the 2.45 lakh panchayats in the country. The project addresses all aspects of panchayats' functioning including planning, monitoring, implementation, budgeting, accounting, social audit and delivery of citizen services like issue of certificates, licenses etc.

Subsequently, e-panchayat scheme was subsumed by Rajiv Gandhi Panchayat Sashaktikaran Abhiyan (RGPSA).

11.8 Kisan Call Centres (KCCs)

The scheme was launched on 21stJanuary 2004 to provide agricultural information to the farming community through toll free telephone lines. A country wide common eleven digit number '1800-180-1551' has been allocated for KCC. The replies to the queries of the farming community are being given in 22 local languages. Calls are attended from 6.00 am to 10.00 pm on all 7 days of the week. In order to make farmers aware of this facility, audio and video spots on Kisan Call Centres are being broadcast telecast through All India Radio/ Doordarshan and private television channels. Kisan Knowledge Management System (KKMS) to provide correct, consistent and quick replies to the queries of farmers is being developed for each State/Union Territory.

11.9 National e-Governance Plan in Agriculture (NeGP-A)

The underlying vision behind this project is to "create an environment conducive for raising farm productivity and income to global levels through provision of relevant information and services to the stakeholders". The initial phase of the project was envisaged to identity the key elements that need to be focused in agriculture and allied sectors. The next phase focused on detailed strategy, roadmap and guidelines for implementation of e-governance in agriculture at both Central and State levels.

There are various IT initiatives/schemes undertaken or implemented by DAC which are aimed at providing information to the farmers on various activities in the agriculture value chain. These initiatives need to be integrated so that farmers may be able to make proper and timely use of the available information. Such information is intended to be provided to farmers through various channels including common service centres, internet kiosks and through SMSs.

11.10 Other IT Services to Agricultural Sector

11.10.1 LAN at Ministry of Agriculture: A high speed local area network was established in the Ministry of Agriculture spread over various buildings viz. Krishi Bhawan (~500 nodes), Shastri Bhawan (~200 nodes), Krishi Anusandhan Bhawan (~100 nodes) etc. In addition, Agricultural Informatics Division has extended its full support (round the clock operation) to the Ministry of Agriculture at the time of super Cyclone in Odisha and Gujarat Earthquake. Video Conferencing facilities were used extensively from the Krishi Bhawan studio to Orissa and Gujarat on continuous basis.

11.10.2 Plant Protection Informatics and Communication Network (PPIN): The PPIN envisages to link the Directorate of Plant Protection Quarantine and Storage (DPPQS), Faridabad, National Plant Protection Training Institute, Hyderabad, CIMPS, LCC, Central Pesticides Testing Laboratories, and State Pesticides Testing Laboratories and to disseminate information related to plant protection and pesticides. As a part of project, the computerization of the CIB/RC of DPPQS has been taken up by NIC.

11.10.3 Agricultural Marketing Information Network (AGMARKNET): NIC has taken up an ambitious project AGMARKNET on turnkey basis for the Directorate of Marketing and Inspection (DMI), Department of Agriculture and Cooperation, Ministry of Agriculture. The project aims at improving the prevailing agricultural marketing information system by minimising the gap between generation and dissemination of market information. The major components of AGMARKNET are the following: (a) establishment of computing facilities and networking, (b) development of human resource, (c) information transmission, (d) development of database, and (e) portal on market information. NIC has tied up with Bharat Sanchar Nigam Ltd. (BSNL) to provide internet facilities at the AGMARKNET nodes.

11.10.4 Strengthening of Informatics in the Offices and Field Units of the Department of Agriculture and Cooperation (DAC)–DACNET: To promote e-governance in Agriculture at the Centre and to provide support to States/UTs for the same, DAC is implementing this Central Sector Scheme. The scheme has the following components:

1. IT apparatus at DAC Headquarters, field offices and Directorates.
2. Development of Agricultural Informatics and Communication.
3. Strengthening of IT Apparatus in Agriculture and Cooperation in the States and Union Territories (AGRISNET).
4. Kisan Call Centres.

11.10.5 MIS Support to Food Processing Industries: To cater to the needs of the Department, NIC has developed various information systems viz. FPO and licensing monitoring, Plan scheme monitoring, industrial approvals, processed food products, FPO on-line status, industrial entrepreneur's memoranda query information, country profile and international cooperation etc.

11.10.6 Agricultural Extension Information System Network: VISTARNET: Research, education, extension, and training are considered as four pillars of sustainable agriculture. Generation and transfer of technology have become very crucial the world over. As a step towards making technology reach the small holders (resource-poor-farmers), efforts are being made to establish VISTARNET-NICNET based Agricultural Extension Information System Network, in India, linking extension functionaries at Central, State, and District level. The required funds for implementing VISTARNET will be provided through the National Agricultural Technology Project (NATP). As a part of VISTARNET, Informatics Development for the Directorate of Extension has been taken up by NIC.

11.10.7 Indian Agriculture Online: NIC has submitted an IT-Plan for the agriculture sector with the objective of establishing NICNET based Agricultural Informatics and Communication Network (AGRISNET) to facilitate higher and sustainable agriculture productivity and also putting Indian Agriculture online in the country.

11.10.8 Infrastructural Facilities and Services Provided by NIC to the Ministry of Agriculture: These are the following:
1. INTRANET/INTERNET.
2. Telecommuting programme.
3. Video conferencing.
4. Information kiosk.
5. In-house training facilities.
6. Website design and development.
7. Web-enabled applications.
8. Information bulletin.
9. Intranet applications.
10. Agriculture portal.
11. NICNET based Public Information and Facilitation Centre.

11.10.9 Animal Production and Health Information Network (APHNET): APHNET envisages building up of reliable databases and network based information systems for all activities of the animal husbandry and dairying sector at district, state and national level, using NICNET facilities. In view of importance of making technology reach the small holders through IT, the plan also suggests to establish APHNET nodes at about 42,000 veterinary polyclinics, hospitals, and dispensaries and veterinary aid centres for strengthening animal disease surveillance and advisory system in the country. As a part of APHNET, National Project on Rinderpest Eradication (NPRE) which aims at capturing animal disease related information from various State Animal Husbandry Departments has been entrusted to NIC.

11.10.10 Agricultural Research Information System Network (ARISNET): The ARISNET, a close user group of institutions in National Agricultural Research System of India (NARS) on NICNET, links ICAR Institutions and their

Regional Research Stations, Central Agricultural University, State Agricultural Universities and their colleges, Krishi Vigyan Kendras, Zonal Research Centres and Project implementing centres with the ICAR Headquarters. ARISNET has become an integral part of agricultural research, extension and education process.

11.10.11 Market Information System for Horticulture: This project has been taken up by NIC on a turnkey basis. As part of the project, NICNET based internet/intranet facilities have been established at National Horticulture Board (NHB), Gurgaon. Computing facilities have been created at 33 market centres of the Board located all over the country. NIC has developed and implemented the necessary software for evolving a comprehensive database of the prices and arrivals of fruits and vegetables being received by NHB headquarters from 33 market centres on a daily basis. This information is being used by the Ministry of Agriculture, its related agencies and markets through National Bulletin on fruits and vegetables.

11.10.12 Integrated Fertilizer Management Information System (FERMIS): The Department of Fertilizers (DOF) in collaboration with National Informatics Centre (NIC) has introduced computer-based methods for decision support with the major objective to evolve an evaluation system which ensures a uniform system of Planning and control mechanism with signalling system to highlight deviations from desired performance indicators by Plants/organisations for all the public sector fertilizer enterprises. Thus, an Integrated Fertilizer Management Information System (IFMIS) of worth ₹ 1.99 crore has been executed through NIC and various IT-based systems developed covering Planning, Movement, Import, Handling-Payment, Project Monitoring, Performance Monitoring and Evaluation aspects to strengthen Fertilizer Informatics for decision support. Information exchange for decision support has been promoted through Fertilizer Informatics Network (FERTNET) extended to Department of Fertilizers and various

Fertilizer Companies viz. IFFCO, NFL, MFL, GNFC, FCI and HFCL.

11.10.13 Activities in the North-Eastern Region: Under the IT apparatus at the Field Offices and Directorates of DAC (DACNET), the following offices in the North-Eastern region have been covered:

1. Directorate of Marketing and Inspection at Guwahati and Shillong.
2. Central Integrated Pest Management Centres at Guwahati, Aizawl, Dimapur and Gangtok.
3. Regional Bio-fertilizer Development Centre at Imphal.
4. North-Eastern Regional Farm Machinery, Testing and Training Institute, Sonitpur, Assam.
5. Support under AGRISNET.

11.11 Computerisation of Agricultural Census and Input Survey

Recognizing the predominance of the agriculture sector in the Indian economy, Department of Agriculture and Cooperation collects and maintains agricultural statistics such as number, area, tenancy, land utilisation, cropping pattern and irrigation particulars of different classes of operational holdings regularly and make it timely accessible to the planners and policy makers for decision making. This project was entrusted to NIC and it made significant headway in almost all the States/UTs except Bihar, where Census is yet to be conducted. The salient features are the following:

1. Creation of large database of about 8,000 million bytes at National Level and 1 GB at state level.
2. Processing and tabulation of Agricultural Census and Input Survey database at District/State/National level.
3. Development and implementation of information retrieval system at micro and macro level for decision-making at various levels.
4. Selective information will be put on internet/intranet for easy access of information to public to ensure transparency

in the Government functioning.
5. Training programmes on software implementation for officers of States/UTs and Central Government.

To sum up, proper planning, monitoring and corrective action requires availability of timely information of right quality. The Central and State Governments require to hasten the process of computerisation of all the records and transactions. Since the government has a major say in promoting agriculture, this will have cascading effect on the entire rural areas. To begin with, it is necessary that the government agencies should accept conventional reports in the electronic format. This will bring about much desired speed and effectiveness in governance.

Many State Governments are showing interest in developing proper systems for e-governance. But the implementation of the same is still requires a lot to be desired. The Central and State Governments should also make information available for ready reference by those interested. This will be not only helpful to people but also will raise interest levels in IT-based services. Similarly, research institutions and NGOs should exchange and provide information through a well conceived network. These measures will encourage end user, i.e. farmer's participation and will provide the much needed input from them.

The face of the Indian agriculture can be transformed by a well conceived deployment of IT. The potential of IT as yet remains untapped and urgent measures are required to derive maximum benefit. The key players involved in this process such as industry, government and educational institutions and research centres are required to make contributions in this endeavour. The initiative to develop necessary IT-based agricultural services need to be developed immediately. Parallel steps to develop necessary IT communication infrastructure are to be taken up along with the utilisation of fibre optic network wherever it is passing through the rural segments.

The Karnataka Government's Bhoomi project has led to the computerisation of the centuries-old system of handwritten rural land records. Through it, the revenue department has done away with the corruption-ridden system that involved bribing village accountants to procure land records; records of right, tenancy and cultivation certificates. The project is expected to benefit seventy lakh villagers in 30,000 villages.

A farmer can walk into the nearest taluk office and ask for a computer printout of his land record certificate for ₹ 15. He can also check details of land records on a touch-screen kiosk by inserting a two-rupee coin. These kiosks, installed at the taluk office, will provide the public with a convenient interface to the land records centre. In this context, the Twelfth Five Year Plan (2012-17) remarked, "Already, a large number of services benefiting ordinary people have come into being. For a small fee, farmers can sign up for a service which provides customer specific information through SMS on market prices in nearby markets, conditions and possible disease outbreaks in specific crops in which the farmer is currently interested. Mobile banking, through business correspondents acting as agents, is giving ordinary people in villages, far from a brick and mortar bank branch, virtually direct access to simple banking service. There is scope for using the Universal Services Obligation Fund (USOF) creatively to enhance access to mobile telephone including especially as a platform for delivery of a range of services to the underserved in rural areas". [1]

Endnote
1. Government of India, Planning Commission, *Twelfth Five Year Plan* (2012-17), Volume I, Chapter 1, para 1.80.

12

India's Cyber Security Policy

Information technology (IT) is one of the critical sectors that rides on and resides in cyber space. It has emerged as one of the most significant growth catalysts for the Indian economy. In addition to fuelling India's economy, this sector is also positively influencing the lives of the people through direct and indirect contribution to the various socio-economic parameters such as employment, standard of living and diversity among others. The sector has played a significant role in transforming India's image to that of a global player in providing world-class technology solutions and IT business services. The government has been a key driver for increases adoption of IT-based products and IT-enabled services.

12.1 What is Cyber Space?

Cyber space is a complex environment consisting of interactions between people, software and services, supported by worldwide distribution of information and communication technology (ICT) devices and networks.

Owing to the numerous benefits brought about by technological advancements, the cyber space is a common pool used by citizens, businesses, critical information infrastructure, military and governments in a manner that makes it difficult to draw clear boundaries among these different groups. The cyber space is expected to be more complex in the foreseeable future, with many-fold increase in networks and devices connected to it.

12.2 Need for Cyber Security

Cyber space is vulnerable to a wide variety of incidents, whether intentional or accidental, man-made or natural, and the data exchanged in the cyber space can be exploited for nefarious purposes by both nation-states and non-state actors. Cyber attacks that target the infrastructure or underlying economic well-being of a nation-state can effectively reduce available state resources and undermine confidence in their supporting structures. A cyber related incident of national significance may take any form: an organized cyber attack, an uncontrolled exploit such as computer virus or worms or any malicious software code, a national disaster with significant cyber consequences or other related incidents capable of causing extensive damage to the information infrastructure or key assets. Large-scale cyber incidents may overwhelm the government, public and private sector resources and services by disrupting functioning of critical information systems. Complications from disruption of such a magnitude may threaten lives, economy and national security.

Rapid identification, information exchange, investigation and co-ordinated response and remediation can mitigate the damage caused by malicious cyber space activity. Some of the examples of cyber threats to individuals, businesses and government are identity theft, phishing, social engineering, activism, cyber terrorism, compound threats targeting mobile devices and smart phone, compromised digital certificates, advanced persistent threats, denial of service, bot nets, supply chain attacks, and data leakages.

12.3 National Cyber Security Policy (NCSP), 2013

NCSP is a policy framework by Department of Electronics and Information Technology (Deity), Ministry of Communication and Information Technology, Government of India. It aims at protecting the public and private infrastructure from cyber attacks. The policy also intends to safeguard "information, such as personal information (of web users), financial and banking information and sovereign data". This was particularly relevant in the wake of US National Security Agency (NSA) leaks that suggested the US government agencies are spying on Indian users, who have no legal or technical safeguards against it.

Ministry of Communications and Information Technology (India) defines cyber space as a complex environment consisting of interactions between people, software services supported by worldwide distribution of information and communication technology.

India had no Cyber security policy before 2013. In 2013, *The Hindu* newspaper, citing documents leaked by NSA whistle blower Edward Snowden, has alleged that much of the NSA surveillance was focused on India's domestic politics and its strategic and commercial interests. This leads to spark furore among people. Under pressure, Government unveiled a National Cyber Security Policy 2013 on July 2, 2013.

Vision: To build a secure and resilient cyberspace for citizens, business and government.

Mission: To protect information and information infrastructure in cyberspace, build capabilities to prevent and respond to cyber threat, reduce vulnerabilities and minimize damage from cyber incidents through a combination of institutional structures, people, processes, technology and cooperation.

12.3.1 Objectives of NCSP: These are as under:

1. To create a secure cyber ecosystem in the country, generate adequate trust and confidence in IT system and transactions in cyberspace and thereby enhance adoption of IT in all sectors of the economy.

2. To create an assurance framework for design of security policies and promotion and enabling actions for compliance to global security standards and best practices by way of conformity assessment (product, process, technology and people).

3. To strengthen the regulatory framework for ensuring a secure cyberspace ecosystem.

4. To enhance and create national and sectoral level 24x7 mechanism for obtaining strategic information regarding threats to ICT infrastructure, creating scenarios for response, resolution and crisis management through

effective predictive, preventive, protective response and recovery actions.

5. To enhance the protection and resilience of nation's critical information infrastructure by operating a 24x7 National Critical Information Infrastructure Protection Centre (NCIIPC) and mandating security practices related to the design, acquisition, development, use and operation of information resources.

6. To develop suitable indigenous security technologies through frontier technology research, solution-oriented research, proof of concept, pilot development, transition, diffusion and commercialization leading to widespread deployment of secure ICT products/processes in general and specifically for addressing national security requirements.

7. To improve visibility of integrity of ICT products and services by establishing infrastructure for testing and validation of security of such product.

8. To create work force for 5,00,000 professionals skilled in next 5 years through capacity building, skill development and training.

9. To provide fiscal benefit to businesses for adoption of standard security practices and processes.

10. To enable Protection of information while in process, handling, storage and transit so as to safeguard privacy of citizen's data and reducing economic losses due to cyber crime or data theft.

11. To enable effective prevention, investigation and prosecution of cyber crime and enhancement of law enforcement capabilities through appropriate legislative intervention.

12. To create a culture of cyber security and privacy enabling responsible user behaviour and actions through an effective communication and promotion strategy.

13. To develop effective public-private-partnerships and collaborative engagements through technical and operational

co-operation and contribution for enhancing the security of cyber space.

14. To enhance global co-operation by promoting shared understanding and leveraging relationships for furthering the cause of security of cyber space.

12.3.2 Strategies of NCSP:

1. Creating a secure cyber ecosystem.
2. Creating an assurance framework.
3. Encouraging open standards.
4. Strengthening the regulatory framework.
5. Creating mechanism for security threat early warning, vulnerability management and response to security threats.
6. Securing e-governance services.
7. Protection and resilience of critical information infrastructure.
8. Promotion of research and development in cyber security.
9. Reducing supply chain risks
10. Human resources development.
11. Creating cyber security awareness.
12. Developing effective public-private-partnership (PPP).
13. Information sharing and co-operation.
14. Prioritized approach for implementation.

A. Creating a Secure Cyber Ecosystem:

- To designate a national nodal agency to co-ordinate all matters related to cyber security in the country, with clearly defined roles and responsibilities.
- To encourage all organizations, private and public to designate a member of senior management as chief information security officer (CISO), responsible for cyber security efforts and initiatives.
- To encourage all organizations to develop information security policies duly integrated with their business plans and implement such policies as per international best practices. Such policies should include establishing standards and mechanisms for secure information flow, crisis management

plan, proactive security posture assessment and forensically-enabled information infrastructure.

- To ensure that all organizations earmark a specific budget for implementing cyber security initiatives and for meeting emergency response arising out of cyber incidents.
- To provide fiscal schemes and incentives to encourage entities to install, strengthen and upgrade information infrastructure with respect to cyber security.
- To prevent occurrence and recurrence of cyber incidents by way of incentives for technology development, cyber security compliance and proactive actions.
- To establish a mechanism for sharing information and for identifying and responding to cyber security incidents and for co-operation in restoration efforts.
- To encourage entities to adopt guidelines for procurement of trustworthy ICT products and provide for procurement of indigenously manufactured ICT products that have security implications.

B. Creating an Assurance Framework:

- To promote adoption of global best practices in information security and compliance and thereby enhance cyber security posture.
- To create infrastructure for conformity assessment and certification of compliance to cyber security best practices, and standards and guidelines.
- To enable implementation of global security best practices in formal risk assessment and risk management processes, business continuity management and cyber crisis management plan by all entities within Government and in critical sectors, to reduce the risk of disruption and improve the security posture.
- To identify and classify information infrastructure facilities and assets at entity level with respect to risk perception for undertaking commensurate security protection measures.
- To encourage secure application/software development processes based on global best practices.

- To create conformity assessment framework for periodic verification of compliance to best practices, standards and guidelines on cyber security.
- To encourage all entities to periodically test and evaluate the adequacy and effectiveness of technical and operational security control measures implemented in IT systems and in networks.

C. Encouraging Open Standards:

- To encourage use of open standards to facilitate interoperability and data exchange among different products and services.
- To promote a consortium of Government and private sector to enhance the availability of tested and certified IT products based on open standards.

D. Strengthening the Regulatory Framework:

- To develop a dynamic legal framework and its periodic review to address the cyber security challenges arising out of technological developments in cyber space and its harmonization with international frameworks including those related to internet governance.
- To mandate periodic audit and evaluation of the adequacy and effectiveness of security of information infrastructure as may be appropriate, with respect to regulatory framework.
- To enable, educate and facilitate awareness of the regulatory framework.

E. Creating Mechanism for Security Threat Early Warning, Vulnerability Management and Response to Security Threats:

- To create national level systems, processes, structures and mechanisms to generate necessary situational scenario of existing and potential cyber security threats and enable timely information sharing for proactive, preventing and protective actions by individual entities.
- To operate a 24x7 National Level Computer Emergency Response Team (CERT) to function as a nodal agency for co-ordination of all efforts for cyber security emergency

response and crisis management.

- To operationalize 24x7 sectoral CERTs for all co-ordination and communication actions within the respective sectors for effective incidence response and resolution and cyber crisis management.
- To implement Cyber Crisis Management Plan for dealing with cyber related incidents impacting critical national processes or endangering public safety and security of the nation, by way of well co-ordinated multi-disciplinary approach at the national sectoral as well as entity levels.
- To conduct and facilitate regular cyber security drills and exercises at national, sectoral and entity levels to enable assessment of the security posture and level of emergency preparedness in resisting and dealing with cyber security incidents.

F. Securing E-governance Services:

- To mandate implementation of global security best practices, business continuity management and cyber crisis management plan for all e-governance initiatives in the country, to reduce the risk of disruption and improve the security posture.
- To encourage wider usage of public key infrastructure (PKI) within government for trusted communication and transactions.
- To engage information security professionals and organizations to assist e-governance initiatives and ensure conformance to security best practices.

G. Protection and Resilience of Critical Information Infrastructure:

- To develop a plan for protection of critical information infrastructure and its integration with business plan at the entity level and implement such plan. The plans shall include establishing mechanisms for secure information flow, guidelines and standards, crisis management plan, proactive security posture assessment and forensically-enabled information infrastructure.

- To operate a 24x7 National Critical Information Infrastructure Protection Centre (NCIIPC) to function as the nodal agency for critical information infrastructure protection in the country.
- To facilitate identification, prioritisation, assessment, remediation and protection of critical infrastructure and key resources based on the plan for protection of critical information infrastructure.
- To mandate implementation of global security best practices, business continuity management and cyber crisis management plan by all critical sector entities, to reduce the risk of disruption and improve the security posture.
- To encourage and mandate as appropriate, the use of validated and certified IT products.
- To mandate security audit of critical information infrastructure on a periodic basis.
- To mandate certification for all security roles to those involved in operation of critical information infrastructure.
- To mandate secure application/software development process based on global best practices.

H. Promotion of Research and Development in Cyber Security:

- To undertake research and development programmes for addressing all aspects of development aimed at short-term, medium-term and long-term goals which include development of trustworthy systems, their testing, deployment and maintenance throughout the life cycle.
- To encourage research and development to produce cost-effective, tailor-made indigenous security solutions meeting a wider range of cyber security challenges and target for export markets.
- To facilitate transition, diffusion and commercialization of the outputs of research and development into commercial products and services for use in public and private sectors.
- To set up centres of excellence in areas of strategic importance for the point of security of cyber space.

- To collaborate in joint research and development projects with industry and academia in frontline technologies and solution-oriented research.

I. Reducing Supply Chain Risks:

- To create and maintain testing infrastructure and facilities for IT security product evaluation and compliance verification as per global standards and practices.
- To build trusted relationships with product/system vendors and service providers for improving end-to-end supply chain security visibility.
- To create awareness of the threats, vulnerabilities and consequences of breach of security among entities for managing supply chain risks related to IT (products, systems or services) procurement.

J. Human Resources Development:

- T foster education and training programmes both in formal and informal sectors to support the nation's cyber security needs and build capacity.
- To establish cyber security training infrastructure across the country by way of public-private-partnership arrangements.
- To establish cyber security concept labs for awareness and skill development in key areas.
- To establish institutional mechanisms for capacity building for law enforcement agencies.

K. Creating Cyber Security Awareness:

- To promote and launch a comprehensive national awareness programme on security of cyber space.
- To sustain security literacy awareness and publicity campaign through electronic media to help citizens to be aware of the challenges of cyber security.
- To conduct, support and enable cyber security workshops/seminars and certifications.

L. Developing Effective Public-Private-Partnership (PPP):

- To facilitate collaboration and co-operation among stakeholder entities including private sector, in the area of cyber security in general and protection of critical information infrastructure in particular for actions related to cyber threats, vulnerabilities, breaches, potential protective measures, and adoption of best practices.

- To create models for collaborations and engagements with all relevant stakeholders.
- To create a think tank for cyber security policy inputs, discussion and deliberations.

M. Information Sharing and Co-operation:

- To develop bilateral and multilateral relationships in the area of cyber security with other countries.
- To enhance national and global co-operation among security agencies, defence agencies and forces, law enforcement agencies and judicial systems.
- To create mechanisms for dialogue related to technical and operational aspects with industry in order to facilitate efforts in recovery and resilience of systems including critical information infrastructure.

N. Prioritized Approach for Implementation:

- To adopt a prioritized approach to implement the policy so as to address the most critical areas in the first instance.

Bibliography

Bibliography

Akella, R. and R. Dossani (2001), "A Report on the Software Value Chain: The Indian Suppliers during the Downturn", Working Paper, Asia-Pacific Research Centre, Stanford University.

Arora, A. and Athreye, S. (2002), "The Software Industry and India's Economics Development", *Information Economics and Policy*, 14(2), 253-273.

Arora, A., V.S. Arunachalam, J. Asundi and F. Ronald (2001), "The Indian Software Services Industry", *Research Policy*, 30(8): 1267-1287.

Athreye, S. (2003), "The Indian Software Industry and its Evolving Service Capability", Working Paper, The Open University, Walton Hall, Milton Keynes, UK.

Athreye, S. (2005), "The Indian Software Industry", in Arora and Gambardella (ed.), 'From Underdogs to Tigers', Oxford University Press: Oxford.

Balakrishnan, P. (2006), "Benign Neglect or Strategic Intent? Contested Lineage of Indian Software Industry", *Economic and Political Weekly*, Vol. 41, No. 36, September 9.

Balasubramanyam, V. and A. Balasubramanyam (2000), "The Software Cluster in Bangalore", in Dunning (ed.), 'Regions, Globalization and the Knowledge-based Economy', Oxford University Press: Oxford.

Basant, Rakesh and Brian Fikkert (1996), "The Effects of R&D, Foreign Technology Purchase, and Domestic and International Spillovers on Productivity in Indian Firms", *Review of Economics and Statistics*, 78(2): 187-200.

Bhattacharya, M. (2004), "Telecom Sector in India: Vision 2020", in 'India Vision 2020', Report of the Committee on India Vision 2020, Planning Commission, Government of India and Background Papers, Academic Foundation, New Delhi.

Chandrasekhar C.P., Jayati Ghosh and Anamitra Roychowdhury (2006), "The Demographic Dividend and Young India's Economic Future", *Economic and Political Weekly*, Vol. 41, No. 49.

Chandrasekhar, C.P. (2006), "The Political Economy of IT-Driven Outsourcing" in Govindan Parayil (ed.), 'Political Economy and

Information Capitalism in India; Digital Divide, Development Divide and Equity', Palgrave Macmillan.

Department of Information Technology (1996), "Guide to Electronics Industry in India", Department of Information Technology, New Delhi.

Dossani, R. and M. Kenney (2002), "Creating an Environment for Venture Capital in India", *World Development*, 30(2), 227-253.

Dunning, J. (1992), "The Competitive Advantages of Countries and the Activities of Transnational Corporations", *Economist*, Innovative India, April 3, 2004, 65-66.

Espenshade, Thomas J. (1999), "High-End Immigrants and the Shortage of Skilled Labour", *Population Research and Policy Review*, Kluwer Academic Publisher, Netherlands.

Government of India, Ministry of Finance, *Economic Survey* (various years).

Government of India, Planning Commission, *Twelfth Five Year Plan* (2012-17).

Hasan, Rana (2002), "The Impact of Imported and Domestic Technologies on the Productivity of Firms: Panel Data Evidence from Indian Manufacturing Firms", *Journal of Development Economics*, 69(1): 23-49.

Heeks, R. (1996), "India's Software Industry: State Policy, Liberalization and Industrial Development", New Delhi, Thousand Oaks, London: Sage Publications.

Hugo, Graeme (2003), "Migration and Development: A Perspective from Asia", Paper prepared for the International Organization for Migration.

Joseph, K.J. (2006), "Information Technology, Innovation System and Trade Regime in Developing Countries: India and the ASEAN", Palgrave Macmillan, London.

Joseph, K.J. (1997), "Industry under Economic Liberalization: The Case of Indian Electronics", New Delhi: Thousand Oaks; London: Sage Publications.

Joseph, K.J. and Vinoj Abraham (2007), "Information Technology and Productivity: Evidence from India's Manufacturing Sector", Working paper No. 389, Centre for Development Studies, Trivandrum.

Joshi, V. (1999), "India's Economic Reforms: 1991-2001", South Asia Books: New Delhi.

Kamibayashi, Cheko (2006), "Current Migration of IT Engineers to

Japan: Beyond Immigration Control and Cultural Barriers", in Christiane Kuptsch and Pang Eng Fong (eds.), 'Competing for Global Talent', ILO and ILLS, Geneva.

Kelkar, V., D. Chaturvedi, and M. Dar (1991), "India's Information Economy: Role, Size and Scope", *Economic and Political Weekly*, September 14, 2153-2160.

Khadria, Binod (1999), "The Migration of Knowledge Workers: Second-Generation Effects of India's Brain Drain", Sage Publications, New Delhi.

Khadria, Binod (2001), "Shifting Paradigms of Globalization: The Twenty-first Century Transition towards Generics in Skilled Migration from India", *International Migration*, Vol. 39(5), Special Issue 1.

Kraemer, K.L. and J. Dedrick (2001), "Information Technology and Economic Development: Results and Policy Implications of Cross-Country Studies", in M. Pohjola (ed.), 'Information Technology, Productivity and Economic Growth', Oxford University Press.

Kripalani, M. and Engardio, P. (2003), "The Rise of India", *Business Week*, December 8.

Kumar, N. and K.J. Joseph (2005), "Export of Software and Business Process Outsourcing from Developing Countries: Lessons from India', *Asia Pacific Trade and Investment Review*, 1(1): 91-108.

Kumar, Nagesh and Aradhna Aggarwal (2005), "Liberalization, Outward Orientation and In-House R&D Activity of Multinational and Local Firms: A Quantitative Exploration for Indian Manufacturing", *Research Policy*, 34(4): 441-460.

Lal, K. (1999), "Determinants of the Adoption of Information Technology: A Case Study of Electrical and Electronic Goods Manufacturing Firms in India", *Research Policy*, 28(7): 667-680.

Mani, S. (2005), "The Dragon vs. the Elephant: Comparative Analysis of Innovation Capability in the Telecommunications Equipment Industry in India and China", Working Paper No. 373, Centre for Development Studies, Trivandrum.

Nagaraj, R. (2004), "Fall in organized Manufacturing Employment: A Note", *Economic and Political Weekly*, July 24, 3387-3390.

NASSCOM (2006), "Study on Domestic Services (IT-ITES) Market Opportunity", National Association of Software and Science Components (Nasscom), New Delhi.

NASSCOM (2006), "The IT Software and Services Industry in India: Strategic Review 2004", New Delhi: National Association of Software and Service Companies.

Nath, P. and A. Hazra (2002), "Configuration of Indian Software Industry", *Economic and Political Weekly*, 37(8): 737-743.

Panagariya, Arvind (2002), "India's Economic Reforms: What Has Been Accomplished? What Remains to be Done?", ERD Policy Brief Series, Economics and Research Department, Asian Development Bank.

Parthasarathi, A., and K. Joseph (2002), "Limits to Innovation in India's ICT Sector", *Science, Technology and Society*, 7(1), 13-50.

Parthasarthy, B. (2006), "The Political Economy of Indian Software Industry", in Parayil G. (ed.), 'Political Economy and Information Capitalism in India: Digital Divide and Equity', Palgrave Macmillan, New York.

Pohjola, M. (2001), "Information Technology and Economic Growth: A Cross-country Analysis" in M. Pohjola (ed.), 'Information Technology, Productivity and Economic Growth', New York: Oxford University Press.

Raut, Lakshmi K. (1995), "R&D Spillover and Productivity Growth: Evidence from Indian Private Firms", *Journal of Development Economics* 48(1): 1-23.

Sen, S. and F. Frankel (2005), "India's Strategy of IT-led Growth", Centre for the Advanced Study of India: Philadelphia, PA.

Upathdya, C., and R.A. Vasavi (2006), "Work, Culture, and Sociality in the Indian IT Industry: A Sociological Study", Final Report submitted to Indo-Dutch Programme for Alternatives in Development, Bangalore.

World Bank (2005), "Project Appraisal Document for an ICT Development", Hanoi, Vietnam.

Index

Index

Bureau (NCRB), 45
National Cyber Security
Policy (NCSP), 2013,
186
National Cyber Security
Policy, 2013, 70
National e-Governance Plan
(NeGP), 84
National e-Governance
Plan in Agriculture
(NeGP-A), 177
National Electronic Funds
Transfer (NEFT), 123
National Exchange for
Automated Trading
(NEAT), 113
National Financial Switch
(NFS), 132
National Informatics
Centre (NIC), 62
National Investigation
Agency (NIA), 44
National Optical Fibre
Network (NOFN), 160
National Optical Fibre
Network Project, 62
National Payments
Corporation of India
(NPCI), 126, 163
National Rural Employment
Guarantee Act Software
Package (NREGASoft),
172
National Securities Clearing
Corporation Ltd
(NSCCL), 109
National Securities
Depositary Ltd. (NSDL),
86, 91, 109
National Stock Exchange

(NSE), 108, 113
National Unified USSD
Platform (NUUP), 166
Negotiated Dealing System
(NDS), 113
Non-profit Governance, 78

O
Online Marketing, 155
Online Tax Accounting
System (OLTAS), 86
Organisation for Economic
Co-operation and
Development (OECD),
81
Over the Counter Exchange
of India (OTCEI),
108, 113

P
Parallel Books of
Accounts, 29
Parallel Economy, 18
Participatory Governance, 79
Participatory Notes, 24
Payment and Settlement
Systems (PSS) Act,
2007, 100
Payment Systems Vision
Document 2012-15, 100
Permanent Account
Number (PAN), 87
*Pradhan Mantri Jan-Dhan
Yojana*, 157
*Pradhan Mantri Garib
Kalyan Deposit Scheme,
2016*, 12
Prevention of Money
Laundering Act (PMLA),
2002, 13, 46